Wall Street's War
With
Middle Class
America

A Thirty Year History

James L. Marsis

and

Dr. DeForest W. Colegrove

Dedication

To our wives, Betty and Ann

Table of Contents

Preface vii

Chapter 1
A Master Plan For An Enduring
Calamity- Introductions 1

Chapter 2
Mergers and Acquisitions- Why Workers Are
Downsized and Corporations
Can't Spare A Dime 27

Chapter 3
Securitization- How Wall Street Cost Millions
of People Their Jobs... 49

Chapter 4
Why It's Not China 75

Chapter 5
Oil- The Story Of How Fuel Fell Under
Wall Street's Control 85

Chapter 6
We Don't Need Two Thousand Pages 131

Bibliography of Books and Articles............................ 145

Preface

Over the last thirty years, American life has been revolutionized by two great changes. The first of these, the computer revolution, is familiar to us all, but the second, the financial revolution, has almost totally escaped the attention it deserves. This is both unfortunate and disturbing because it's this second phenomenon, the morphing of New York investment banks into multilayered mega-banks, that has reversed the fortunes of the once-prosperous American middle-class.

Despite the importance of this change, these new super-banks have received very little attention. It was only in 2007/2008, when their dangerous bets brought down the entire global economy, that they were covered with any real consistency. Yet, even here, the catastrophic fall they triggered was treated as an isolated event rather than an as outgrowth of the changes that have been reshaping the nation's financial structure over the last three decades. Despite the fact that the activities of New York's huge banks are connected to the current struggles of the middle-class, these institutions have managed to pose as mere sideline players, largely unrecognized as the powerbrokers that they have become.

Those old enough to remember how our financial system used to operate appreciate that something has gone very wrong. However, because news reporting rarely follows long-term trends, it's not possible for people pursuing their daily lives to fashion a coherent picture of what has really happened. Day-to-day reporting of isolated financial news has simply not been able to do the job. Ironically, even though we are bombarded with a never ending stream of information, the public has completely missed Wall Street's takeover of the American economy.

There are, of course, books that have been written on the global meltdown, and a decade or two ago, there were a few that reported on the hostile takeover movement that Wall Street engineered. Nevertheless, to our knowledge nothing has been written which places events such as these within the context of a revolution that is causing the demise of the American middle-class. To date, there hasn't even been a systematic study on the effects of Wall Street's takeover of the global oil markets, even though this newest area of activity is keeping the price of gasoline in the area of $2/gallon higher than it should be. A power grab has taken place right under our noses but it has gone almost completely unreported.

Hollywood, which rarely fails to pick up on deep economic and social trends, has caught the spirit of what's going on. Oliver Stone, in creating his character, Gordon Gecko, has succeeded in fashioning the archetype of the new spirit of greed that now embodies the operatives of our financial system. Nevertheless, even in this provocative film, Gecko, this "Darth Vader" of Stone's, *Wall Street,* is viewed as an isolated figure. It's probable that most people who saw this film left the movie feeling relieved that they had escaped the dealings of a man like this. The problem is no one has. We are all in Gecko's cross-hairs now. New York should be our focus, not China. As this book will explain, Wall Street, for average Americans, is the true source of our real economic misgivings.

IN COMPOSING THIS book, we have made every effort to write it in a non-technical style so that its contents can be easily followed by the general public. It's our sincerest hope that it ignites some of the indignation we all should be feeling.

AS IS THE case with most books, the list of people who extended their help and encouragement is a long one, but we would like to single out Ellen O'Brien, Carolyn Testa, and Joseph Lorenzo for their patient help, as well as Laurie Duffy, Josie Banks, and Ann Colegrove for their work in helping with the editing of this book. We would also like to extend our heartfelt thanks to each of our wives, Ann Colegrove and Betty Marsis for the constant encouragement and support they lent.

Chapter 1.

A Master Plan
For An Enduring
Calamity- Introductions

*In our managerial age, evil is not
conceived in concentration camps;
it is the final result of quiet words
spoken by well dressed men in
carpeted offices.*
Margaret P. Hannay's paraphrase of
C.S.Lewis' The Screwtape Letters

How Three New Approaches To Making Money Produced A Revolution

Wall Street makes too much money. Its investment banks and hedge funds make so much money in fact that the financial sector's total share of the nation's profits now hovers just slightly under 50%. Think of that. Nearly half of all corporate profits are no longer going to companies that make things. Rather, they are being redirected to institutions that buy and sell financial paper. And all of this is recent. In 1950, Wall Street's share of all corporate profits was a mere 8%, only one-sixth of their current level.[1]

Forty years ago, investment banks operated on a very modest scale, and with modest ambitions. They did what they were expected to do, which is to transfer capital from people who have it to lend to those who need it and don't have it.[2] This, of course, is still supposed to be their basic function, but, unfortunately, it no longer is. Since the 1980's, investment banks have found new and very profitable ways of operating, utilizing schemes that allow quick fortunes to be made. If in turn these operations are actually of benefit to the economy as well as to themselves, then that's a plus. But if profits are being made at the public's expense, then that's okay too, for this group now operates with a new set of values, values premised on the idea that individual interests trump those of the larger society.

THE GENERATION THAT came of age in the 1970's, the one that turned our college campuses upside down, is the one that developed the attitudes now prevalent on Wall Street.[3] When members of this

1   Kevin Phillips, *Bad Money: Reckless Finance, Failed Politics, and the Global Crises of American capitalism,* Viking-The Penguin Group, 2008. See the graph on p. 31.

2   For an excellent discussion on the limited role that investment banks played in the 1950's, see John Kenneth Galbraith, *The New Industrial State,* Boston, Houghton-Mifflin, 3rd. ed. 1967.

3   Michael Lewis, *The Big Short,* New York: W.W. Norton & Co., 2010, p. xviii

group moved on into finance, they quickly showed an unwillingness to simply settle for making a good living. What they wanted was to be rich, rich actually beyond imagining. For men like Michael Milken, Carl Icahn and Ivan Boesky, all of whom came of age in the 1960's and 70's, it became necessary to count their wealth in billions. Millions were no longer enough. They wanted to be billionaires and they clearly saw that the old ways of doing business, such as managing portfolios and limiting themselves to executing the sale of stocks and bonds would never get them there. So they created nontraditional ways of doing things, employing methods that could bring them riches by squeezing huge sums out of corporations, and out of consumers, and even out of each other. Here is a brief look at the three new areas of activity that men like Milken created, revolutionary activities that would earn them fortunes, and change forever the way Wall street did business.

IF WE FOLLOW these developments chronologically, the change began when investment banks, led by Michael Milken, realized just how easy it was to seize control of a corporation and to then use this control to vote themselves huge dividends. It was Milken's work with mergers and acquisitions in the 1980's that first began to shift wealth out of the mainstream economy and into the coffers of New York banks. Corporate take-overs, often hostile in their execution, are what first made billionaires in finance common-place.

The next "creative" group, led by Louis Ranieri, also emerged in the 1980's. It was Ranieri who cooked up the idea of bundling mortgages into large securities that could be sold to banks throughout the world. Ranieri's idea eventually spread to every conceivable type of consumer loan. Sometimes called "asset-backed securities", these new "instruments" allowed individual traders to make fortunes on commissions as banks sold them to each other in amounts worth trillions of dollars. These are the securities that by late 2007 had dried up useful capital, leaving the money needed for legitimate corporate loans all but gone. Asset backed securities soaked up useful capital like a sponge, and when everything finally did collapse, banks had to be supplied with money from the Treasury and the Federal Reserve in order to continue their loan operations. The Fed, feeling it has no choice, is still pouring money into the system, hoping that the bad paper that remains with the banks will eventually be washed away.

Mergers and acquisitions, along with asset-backed securities, made fortunes for investment banks. It's what made those huge profits we alluded to earlier. By late 2008, however, banks like Goldman Sachs, as well as a number of hedge funds felt it necessary to search for new markets because the asset-backed securities they had created had taken down all of their usual areas of investment. Dot coms, real estate, currencies, they were all down. So the big players turned to a market they had never ventured into before. They moved into petroleum. In 2008, they entered the oil markets in droves.

The base of operations for major investments in oil had been established in New York in the 1990's. In that decade, some minor speculators had developed a small trade in oil, mostly with small home fuel oil companies, buying and selling futures on the relatively new New York Mercantile Exchange.[4] But until 2008, the major banks and hedge funds had given this market little attention. They had been making fortunes elsewhere. After the global meltdown, however, things were different. They needed a new market. Mostly by using complex financial contracts called derivatives, they began to manipulate the global demand for oil. Even though the demand for petroleum was reeling with the global recession, prices shot up within a couple of months as the demand placed by New York's big banks and hedge funds did its work. Within weeks, the price of oil went from $24/barrel to $147/barrel. Eventually, prices settled in the area of $90/barrel, where they continue to hover today. At this price, a gallon of gasoline costs approximately $2 more per gallon than it otherwise would. It is this newly acquired control of the oil markets that have completed Wall Street's strangle hold on the American economy.

Through hostile takeovers and the sale of asset backed securities, and by the seizure of most of the

---

4   Emily Lambert, *The Futures, The Rise of the Speculator and the Origins of the World's Biggest Markets,* New York: Basic Books, The Perseus Book Group, 2011, p. 49.

world's oil markets, New York has successfully closed its noose around our economy, and around the pocketbooks of the middle class. We will examine these three gambits in detail in the chapters that follow. In the present chapter, we will look at the effects that finance's new way of doing business has had on the incomes of both Wall Street and Main Street. This present chapter will also try to fathom what's motivating this present generation of financiers.

Exactly How Much Are They Making?

We've mentioned that the financial sector's profits have risen to 50% of the entire economy's profits, but we've yet to mention the kind of money that's being made by individuals in the industry. The incomes that individual financiers are making are as staggering as their total profit figure is.

Let's start with the hedge fund manager who's announced his earnings for 2011 were $5 billion dollars. Five billion dollars is five thousand million dollars. How does $5 billion earned in a single year compare with the bloated salaries we complain about with our professional athletes? When a very successful baseball player earns $20 million in a single year, the figure causes an outcry. And yet, our baseball player would have to play for 250 years to earn what our hedge fund manager earned in one. Or take the case of John Paulson, an oft lionized New York hedge fund manager. He helped to push the market over the cliff in 2008 by betting against the sub-prime mortgage bonds that were threatening to bankrupt Citigroup and other investment banks. For his efforts in helping to ruin the entire global economy, Paulson personally made $4 billion, while his group of investors made another $20 billion.[5] To the ordinary citizen, whose median income hovers around $50,000/year, it's an incomprehensible display of selfishness and greed. At a $50,000 annual income, it would take the average family eighty thousand years to make what Paulson made in one.

Although most Americans are unaware of the magnitude of the incomes that are being made at the top, they are aware that something is wrong. That's why the political rhetoric of class warfare is so effective. It should be taken as an early warning signal of the deeper potential rumblings that may be coming.

Now let's take a look at Paulson's colleagues. Consider the fact that while Paulson was making his fortune, fifty other hedge fund managers were earning, in a single year, enough to exceed the paychecks of more than nine million working Americans.[6] What fifty hedge fund managers earned in a single year amounted to more than what 15% of what the entire American labor force earned, and this in an industry that forty years ago was so small that hedge funds were irrelevant.

---

5   Lewis, *The Big Short, p. xviii*

6   Matt Miller, *The Tyranny Of Dead Ideas: Letting Go Of The Old Ways Of Thinking To Unleash A New Prosperity.* New York: Henry Holt and Company, 2009, pp. 140-141.

Here's one last tale that helps to capture what's going on. It's the story of a small time trader who buys and sells oil on the New York Mercantile Exchange (NYMEX). In a book entitled Rigged, Ben Mezrich tells the story of Michael Vitzioli, who after making a $500,000 profit in one morning, threw a big party in the VIP section of a hip night club in the "flatiron" district of Manhattan.[7] Mike's party, he notes, flowed well into the morning hours with an abundance of champagne, vodka and women. The waitress, Mezrich says, "nearly fainted when Vitzioli ordered that twelfth bottle of Crystal champagne. For Vitzioli, it was simply one of many shows that are put on to celebrate a good day on the Street.

Just how many tales of greed are there to tell? The list is too long to catalog. What we've cited are merely examples of an industry that is out of control. When the once staid investment bank, Goldman Sachs, comes to be described as a "vampire squid" by one of its former employees, we know that the problem is woven into the system.[8] Perhaps an anecdote told by columnist Matt Miller sums the whole situation up best. Miller notes that he was recently told by an investment banker worth $80 million that he wasn't in banking for the money. If he was, he notes, "I'd be at a hedge fund".

---

7   Ben Mexrich, *Rigged: The True Story Of An Ivy League Kid Who Changed The World Of Oil*, New York: William Morrow, 2007, pp. 3-5.

8   See Greg Smith, *Why I Left Goldman Sachs: A Wall Street Story*. New York: Grand Central Publishing, 2012.

Miller's reaction to this was to suggest that "only on a small plot of real estate on lower Manhattan at the dawn of the twenty-first century could such a statement be remotely fathomable. That it is suggests how debauched our ruling class has become...."[9]

Whose Bearing The Cost For All This?

Unlike Matt Miller, most economists shy away from discussing the problem, but the fact remains that there is an inverse relationship between the earning trends of finance and that of average working Americans. As the earnings of the financial sector increase, the earnings of the middle class decrease. The big money that is being made is coming from the pockets of average people because the top and the middle are bound together in a see-saw relationship. The decline in middle class incomes that we are currently experiencing is in perfect step with the rise of Wall Street's prosperity.

Not all would agree. It's commonly suggested, for example, that the country's growing inequality is linked to the increasing demands that technology is placing on education. There is a standard argument which holds that in a computerized society, good jobs, and even moderately paying jobs, now require a college degree. The argument asserts that it is this situation that is causing our non-college groups to sink, even while our college graduates are prospering. Just recently, Francis Fukuyama, a senior fellow at Stanford University,

---

9   Miller, *The Tyranny Of Dead Ideas*, p. 131.

published an article reiterating this theme in the journal, *Foreign Affairs*. In his piece, Fukuyama notes that

> the benefits of the most recent waves
> of technological innovation have
> accrued disproportionately to the
> most talented and well educated
> members of society . . . . Every
> great advance for Silicon Valley
> likely means the loss of low skilled
> jobs elsewhere.[10]

Fukayama goes on to state that differences in talent, character, ambition and the like have always produced inequality, but today it has become magnified by the appearance of a new technology.

Is there any truth to this "techno-education" argument? Yes, of course there is. As proof, we can point to towns and cities where older industries have returned, bringing with them the old style prosperity that non-college workers all once enjoyed. The problem is explanations like these all fall far short of a complete explanation. It's a question of magnitude. Yes, educated groups do better than non-educated groups, and the return of older style smoke-stack industries on a large scale would help to close the gap. But even if this gap were closed, it doesn't mean that the problem of a poorly performing middle class

---

10   Francis Fukuyama, "The Future of History: Can Liberal Democracy Survive the Decline of the Middle Class", *Foreign Affairs*, January/February, 2012.

would disappear. For the truth is that even the advantages that a college degree generates are not enough. The education argument gives the impression that college grads are doing well when if fact they are not. If we peel away the layers that separate college graduates themselves, we find that education is not nearly as important in explaining middle class stagnation as it would at first appear to be. Consider the following numbers. Over the last thirty years, college graduates have increased their incomes by a paltry 25%. That's less than one percent a year, not nearly enough to cover the rise in expenses that maturity brings. If the comparative figures look good, it's only because those with less than a college degree are doing so poorly. The chart below gives a much clearer picture of what real US income trends have been.

Cumulative Income Gains By Educational Level[11]

	Less Than HS	High School	College	Top 1%
1980	---------------------- base year----------------------			
1990	-20%	-10%	+8%	+70%
1995	-25%	-10%	+9%	+65%
2000	-25%	-7%	+15%	+150%
2005	-22%	0%	+25%	+150%
2007	-20%	0%	+27%	+275%

---

11   "The Rich Get Richer,""American Educator, Vol 36, No. 1, Spring 2012, p.3 . See also, "There's More To Inequality Than Education.", www.EPI.org/blog/inequality-education.

There is a simple rule which states that a 1% yearly increase in incomes will lead to a doubling of purchasing power every 72 years through compounding. If we apply this rule of 72 to the above figures, we can see just how significantly income changes over the last thirty years have affected Americans from top to bottom.

- The top 1%, since they have increased their incomes by roughly 10%/year, have doubled their purchasing power every 7.2 years.
- College grads, since they have increased their incomes by roughly 1%/year, have doubled their purchasing power every 72 years.
- High School grads- since they have had no gains at all have been completely stagnate for a generation, in a world where housing, food, fuel and medical costs are all rising
- Less than high school- they have suffered a loss of 25% of their purchasing power over the last thirty years.

In an op-ed piece in the *Wall Street Journal*, Sean Fieler presents the same picture by noting that if we use 1971 as a base year, when median incomes are adjusted for inflation, the national figure of $50,000 becomes reduced to $9,000.[12] This reduces median household income increases over four decades to a

---

12   Sean Fieler, "Easy Money Is Punishing The Middle Class", *The Wall Street Journal, September 27, 2012, p. A19.*

mere 12%.[13] Over a forty year period, this figure represents an increase of 1/3 of 1% a year, and this says nothing about the essentials that have outpaced average inflation. By focusing on inflation, Fieler essentially gives the same picture as does the chart based on education. The middle class has been stagnant for the last four decades, including nearly all of its college graduates, the very people who can master technology. So is it really any wonder that the welfare state continues to grow, and that the rhetoric of class warfare grows along with it?

These Are A New Breed Of Cats

Trying to understand life through theories always runs head on against thorny obstacles such as history, chance, and unaccountable personal motives. Still, it's impossible not to ask why the present generation of people working on Wall Street has such an obsession with making money. Where did their "take no prisoners" approach come from, and why do they all want to be as rich as the legendary King Croesus?

We will try to explain the emergence of finance's quest for wealth by looking briefly at both the ideas and the institutions that emerged around the time that our present day financiers were coming of age. For example, could it be that values have changed simply because hedge funds have shown that making a great fortune is possible? Seeing that something can be done is bound to draw the attention of others

13   Ibid.

in the field. Perhaps being able to do it was all the push that was needed to change the system. But there are writers who would offer alternative explanations. Both Michael Lewis and Matt Taibii have suggested that the causes run deeper.[14] They both believe a revolution in ideas has occurred, a revolution which had a particular appeal to the boomer generation because they were very susceptible to new and radical ways of thinking. There was a lot bubbling under the surface in the 1950's, when hedge funds and radical philosophy first made their way into the American consciousness. These were undercurrents that continued to percolate until they became a strong brew for the young and rebellious generation of the 1960's. For this was a group that had never known hardship and that was greatly attached to novelty.

Hedge Funds

Is the very existence of these institutions the key to understanding shifting values? One would think that they have played a role simply by the example they set because they are the major movers and shakers of the new financial markets. Given their huge profits, they now set the example for others to emulate.

In this new age of finance, there is nothing that represents the new Wall Street culture more than

14   Micharl Lewis, *The Money Culture*, New York: Penguin Books. See also Matt Taibbi, *Griftopia, Bubble Machines, Vampire Squids, and the LongCon That Is Breaking America*, New York: Spiegel&Grow, New York, 2010.

hedge funds. No other institutions, not even our biggest banks, demonstrate a love for moneymaking like the hedge funds do. These funds, which were relatively unimportant before the 1990's, now represent the richest, smartest, and most grasping of all financial institutions- which is saying a lot when one considers the recent performance of banks like Goldman Sachs.

HEDGE FUNDS ARE private, exclusive investment "clubs," almost totally unregulated. They invest huge sums of money which have been loaned to them by banks, corporations, state treasuries, and wealthy individuals. Their name comes from the investment strategy they employ, which is to "hedge" their bets by using a combination of both buying and selling. They will, for example, buy some stocks "long," hoping the price rises, while at the same time hedging their bet by selling other stocks "short". Selling short means they will borrow securities like stocks from banks, insurance companies or whomever, and sell them, with the promise to buy them back before a specified date. They are, in effect, betting the market, or at least the securities they are selling, will fall in price by the time they buy them back. In this way they cover themselves for whatever movement the market takes. But it's a complex operation, with those securities that are bought long and those that are sold short being guided by complex formulas. Because the people who manage hedge funds are the best in the business, hedge funds have been phenomenally successful.

Besides talent and the strategy of hedging, hedge funds are really defined by the massive leveraging (borrowing) they use. Most of what they do is with borrowed money and securities.

As it turns out, playing with other people's money can be extraordinarily profitable, as well as dangerous. Here's why. Let's say, for example, you manage a hedge fund and borrow $99 million in order to buy some Ford stock. You also put up $1 million of your own money as well, so that your total investment comes to $100 million. If this investment makes a 1% return, raising the value of your stock to $101 million, that $1 million in profit is equal to the $1 million you put up out of your fund's capital. That means you've made a 100% profit, even though the total investment has only returned 1%. This capacity both to win big and to threaten the stability of global markets by losing big is what makes these funds explosively profitable as well as dangerous.

The ability to leverage this way is the most important characteristic of hedge funds. It allows them to generate enormous sums, which is why they are so powerful. Because they move billions of dollars when they go either long or short, they can influence the way the markets will move simply by the momentum their activity generates. All the hedge funds watch what the biggest of their group is doing because the giants will oftentimes deliberately commit their huge resources in order to establish a momentum in the direction they want. The smaller funds will then tag along.[15] This is what they did with oil in 2008, when they sent it from \$34/barrel to \$147/barrel, and then back down to \$35, all within a six month period.

So it's certainly possible that hedge funds have played a role in shifting the values of Wall Street simply because they've shown that becoming super rich is within the grasp of a very talented few.

When the system was more guarded and returns more moderate, people acted with moderation. It was easy for honor, honesty, integrity and humility to flourish. But given new possibilities, the young financiers' thinking seems to have adjusted to what's now become possible. The causes of cultural shifts are usually subtle, but in the case of hedge funds, they came as a thunder clap.

HEDGE FUNDS HELPED to change our values because they showed how immense wealth could be made. But there are probably other factors too that have shifted the thinking of lower Manhattan.

Michael Lewis, a writer who worked on Wall Street, sees the value shift as being connected to the counter-culture revolution of the 60's, that era when college students declared war on everything American, from values, and institutions, to rules and standards of behavior. All one has to do to catch the flavor of those turbulent times is to read a snippet

---

15   See especially interviews of leading hedge fund managers in Steven Drobny, *Inside The House of Money*, Hoboken, New Jersey: John Wiley and Sons, 2009.

of Jack Kerouac's *On the Road*,[16] or watch a portion of the 1960's movie, *Easy Rider*. Each comes from different directions but they make the point. The old rules were under attack.

The Woodstock generation, and all it represented, is what Michael Lewis is alluding to. As Lewis sees it, today's firms are run by counter-culture hippies who now have a real chance to wreak the havoc they have always wanted to on the values and institutions they have always despised. Making money, he says, actually means very little to them. It's simply a way of keeping score.[17]

Does Lewis' explanation correlate with ours in explaining the power of hedge funds? It would seem so, for these institutions have made it all possible for a group that loathes tradition, to turn traditional values on their head. Hedge funds are a vehicle of choice for attacking the old, staid values of earlier bankers.

Matt Taibbi is another writer, whose work is very suggestive. Taibii has attempted to explain Wall Street's "orgiastic" chase after wealth by concluding that the problem lies with a philosophy that stresses the primacy of the individual over the group. He sees the problem originating from a belief system that

---

16   Jack Kerouac, *On the Road*, New York: The Viking Press, 1957.

17   Michael Lewis, *Liar's Poke: Rising Through the Wreckage on Wall Street*, New York: Penguin Books, 1990, Preface.

removes all personal restraint, weakening the values nurtured by family, church, and nation.[18]

At the center of Taibbi's argument sits Alan Greenspan, a man who served as Federal Reserve Chairman under four presidents. Greenspan, he argues, has spread the philosophy of avarice throughout New York in much the same way that typhoid Mary spread that illness in the same city a hundred years earlier. Taibbi maintains that Wall Street has been overtaken by an offshoot of post-War libertarianism, a sort of pleasure-based philosophy that ultimately focuses on money. This philosophy owes its origins to Ayn Rand, a Russian émigré who wrote influential novels in the 50's and who served as a college instructor to the young Greenspan. Even if Rand's role is exaggerated, she's still very representative of all that is new. It's worth taking a closer look at her.

Ayn Rand - A Voice For A New Era

Born in 1905, Ayn Rand, even as a child, hated the mysticism and collectivism of Czarist Russia. Later, she came to hate the doctrines of communism as well, but she was spared the suffocating environment of Bolshevism when as a young woman teaching history at the University of Petersburg she was granted a temporary visa to do research in the US. She left the USSR and never returned. Instead, she showed up in New York, taught at Columbia, and wrote two famous novels which extolled a philosophy of radical

---

18   See Taibbi, *Griftopia.*.

individualism.[19] Both of these works were popular with America's avant guard and with the young generally because to an inexperienced life they provided an exciting new formula to live by. For young people, whose lives are still free of the contradictions and complexities that make older people suspicious of ideology, Rand was an exciting breath of fresh air.

Greenspan crossed paths with Ayn Rand at just such a young age, when he took classes with her at Columbia. It's said that if anyone in Rand's class merely mentioned the idea of a moral order, they would be met with laughter from everyone in the class, including the professor. Apparently Rand had forgotten what it was that she hated at the University of Petersburg as she took the religious intolerance of the left and made it the standard for her personal creed.

In Taibbi's interpretation, Rand's ideas were passed from Greenspan to Wall Street, first in his tenure as a top investment banker and then, from his high perch as the Chairman of the Federal Reserve. The "Maestro" became, for Taibbi, the secular equivalent of a religious zealot, spreading a new teaching that could be

---

19   See Ayn Rand, *Atlas Shrugged, published by Plume, a member of Penguin Putnum Group, 1957* and *The Fountainhead, The Bobbs-Merrill Co., 1943.*. For a less popular but very revealing title, see also *The Virtue of Selfishness,* Signet Printing, 1948.

accurately described as ethical self-centeredness or more simply as selfishness.[20]

There's no doubt that such a connection is reasonable, but whether Wall Street lost its moral compass because of Greenspan, or simply because a new ethic was in the air will remain unknowable. Either way, Rand does stand as the archetype of a new, self-centered morality that is against all state imposed regulation of the market place. If Taibii is only partially right, if her works are not explicitly the guiding spirit of present day finance, then at the least, they are implicitly, for, Greenspan, one of her inner circle, rose to the highest levels of control in the US financial system. As Chairman of The Fed, it was Greenspan who continually fed banks with all the money they needed when the bond market collapsed in the early 90's, and when the dot-com bubble burst later in the decade, signaling that losses from reckless speculation would be covered by the government. It was also Greenspan who shut down Brooksly Bourne when she warned that the unregulated derivatives market could pull down the entire global economy. Because his role was so pivotal in the crucial decade of the 90's, he merits a closer look.

AS A YOUNG man, Greenspan became a member of Rand's inner circle, a group that called itself "The Collective," a rather odd name for a group that worshiped hyper-individualism. As a member of this collective, the future "banker-chairman" was in a position to imbibe every detail of Rand's thought.

---

20   Taibbi, *Griftopia,*. p. 39.

Her system, which is termed "objectivist philosophy," could have been called, as Taibbi suggests, "Greedism," but that wouldn't have offered the pizzazz that the more technical term does.[21] Hence, objectivist philosophy is the term that we use.

What objectivist philosophy stands for is the idea that any interference with what benefits one's own self-interest is an evil. Recall that the title of one of Rand's work is *The Virtue of Selfishness.*[22] With a title like this it's not hard to see that we are being presented with an opinion that could never be reconciled with core group values that place the individual within the context of a larger group. Here we are presented with a blanket rejection of anything that interferes with self-gratification. For Rand, there is nothing larger than oneself. Rand's system sees ethics and self-interest as one and the same. A grasping life is a self-fulfilling life. In Rand's words,

> "Man does not live on a raft with one
> bottle of water. He lives on earth,
> which gives him infinite resources-
> and it is up to him to get them. His
> proper conduct and morality must be
> based on this fact."[23]

---

21   Ibid. p. 39.

22   Ayn Rand, *The Virtue of Selfishness,* New York: Signet Publishers, 1963

23   "Letter To Rose Wilder Lane", *Letters of Ayn Rand,* a Dutton Book, 1995, p.354.

Here was a call to the young Greenspan to practice finance for the single minded purpose of becoming rich. If in the process he could foster the prosperity of the nation, that would be fine too, but maximizing his own prosperity came first.

IF TAIBBI'S JUDGEMENT seems harsh, it nevertheless remains true that as the powerful chairman of the Federal Reserve for so many years, Greenspan pursued policies that made him an enabler as he pumped dollars into the banking system he once worked for in such explosive amounts that financiers quickly learned that they could make fortunes by using this money to drive up dot-com stock values, mortgage values, and derivatives to levels that had no relationship to reality. Best of all, for Wall Street, when these bubbles burst, there was no downside in New York, because bailout money was quickly pumped back into the system by the Fed. Since the collapse in 2008, we've been treated to many picturesque Rand moments as banks received trillions from the Fed at essentially 0% interest and promptly sent this interest-free money to European banks which paid them a hefty return. The fact that small businesses desperately need loans here at home meant little and continues to mean little.

It's the middle class who have paid for these Rand- like investments. They've watched their pensions get damaged, their home values fall, and have lost 16 million jobs that still have not been replaced. Meanwhile, the millions continue to pour into Wall

Street salaries. If this self-serving behavior isn't criminal, then it's only because of those who define criminality. It's chilling to think that these are the ethics that our financial sector subscribes to.

WHAT WALL STREET does is usually defended under the banner of capitalism, the free market system that's made this nation so prosperous. Nothing could be less true. Capitalism sees profits as the reward for a job well done, not as the result of the successful manipulation of the system. The derivatives markets which are a hedge fund specialty have drained many state treasuries and corporate portfolios by selling them obscure contracts that had little or no chance of making money![24] This is simply theft, which has nothing to do with capitalism.

Big banks and hedge funds made and continue to make fortunes on securities and derivatives that never have the real value they are being sold for.

> those oil futures were never
> close to being worth $140/barrel,
> [but the] fees that went to Goldman
> Sachs and Morgan Stanley did get
> turned into real beach houses....[25]

---

24   Frank Portnoy, a derivatives salesman, makes the point that hedge funds constantly snooker state treasuries, because they are run by people lacking top experience. See Frank Portnoy, *Fiasco: Blood in the Water on Wall Street*, New York: W.W. Norton, 2009.

25   Taibbi, *Griftopia*, pp. 52-53

HAS THIS REMARKABLE chase after wealth really put the middle class in survival mode? In a word, yes! The new financial environment we find ourselves in has ended a thirty year run of middle class prosperity and brought us to our current period represented by thirty years of stagnation. Our current financial structure has turned middle America, which was once filled with a sense of buoyancy and forward motion, into a group that is overworked and that is constantly fighting to keep its standard of living from falling. The heavy credit card debt which so many families now find themselves straddled with is not the result of some new found extravagance. It's mostly the result of an attempt to keep up. In recent surveys, two-thirds of the middle class now indicate that they believe their future standard of living will decline.[26] What economists once called "the golden age of capitalism" has been brought to an end by a group of financiers who feel it is a moral good to recklessly pursue their self-interest, and who, in addition, believe it is an evil to interfere with this pursuit, regardless of the consequences the rest of society is forced to live with.

A Synthesis

So we have hedge funds playing a role, and both Michael Lewis, and Matt Taibii offering insights into Wall Street's changed behavior. Taking the three

---

26   Peggy Noonan, "The Tea Party Movement," op.ed. page, *Wall Street Journal*, October 23, 2010. .

together, what we have is counter culture hippies who are now dressed in suits and who are armed by a philosophy that justifies unethical behavior. All of this certainly seems plausible but perhaps there's something even more obvious. The whole venture of amassing more wealth than anyone could use seems childish. There are those who have their agendas, such as George Soros, but in the main, this is money being made simply for making money. Fully matured adults are usually more temperate than that, and are usually more prudent and thoughtful as well. Continued overindulgence and thoughtlessness, neglecting to consider the possible consequences of what we do are the traits of children. It's a strange notion that the chief movers of our society may be operating in a frozen state of adolescence, but we may very well be living in a culture where many people are reluctant to leave their adolescence behind, because those years are, after all, when accountability is at a minimum.

$

Chapter 2.
Mergers and Acquisitions-Why Workers are Downsized and Corporations Can't Spare a Dime

*Private companies no longer exist
to serve the state and provide jobs;
they answer to a demanding bunch of
private investors whose main concern
is profits.*
Thomas Friedman, *The Lexus and the Olive Tree*

Wall Street Comes Out of the Shadows-
If we consider the long run impact that Wall Street has had on the American economy and its workers, the most damaging of all of its recent creations has been the emergence of the modern corporate takeover movement. Known also as "mergers and acquisitions", this activity has allowed the financial sector to gain complete ascendancy over corporate America, changing its very character in a revolutionary way, and in the process, seriously penalizing the American worker.

Nothing Wall Street has done in the last three decades has harmed the middle class more than this movement has because corporate takeovers have forced the replacement of a relatively benign corporate culture with one that is completely rapacious. In modern corporate thinking, no one's interests except those of shareholders are of any consequence. The interests of both managers and on-line workers no longer enter into policy decisions. Mergers and acquisitions have forced boardrooms to focus exclusively on shareholder dividends. This is why quarterly profit projections have become so important. If these projections are in danger of not being met, wages will be squeezed, hours worked lengthened, and if necessary, workers downsized, even if the company is making a profit. This was unheard of in the 1950's and 60's, but as we all know, it's now an everyday occurrence. CEO's have no other option because if they don't play ball, they'll soon find themselves out in the street. In the corporations of the US, securing quarterly dividends for the company's shareholders is the reason why the corporation exists. It's such a common way of thinking that many would now respond by asking, why else would a corporation exist? In Europe and Japan today, and in post-World War II America, the answer would have been that it exists for the welfare of everyone.

Recall this chapter's opening quote by Thomas Friedman, which points out, that "corporations no longer exist to serve their society, or the workers that run them. They exist to serve a new master." It's a revolutionary transition that Friedman is pointing to, and it has been brought about by the power that mergers and acquisitions have given banks over corporate America. What's particularly vexing is the fact that this activity has forced the replacement of a system that had produced unrivaled worker prosperity. Mergers and acquisitions replaced an era that economists now nostalgically refer to as "The Golden Age of Capitalism."

This dramatic change in the way our nation does business inevitably leads to the question of, how did this all start? Most significant changes in a society usually evolve, or at the very least, have their groundwork slowly laid so that we can see them coming. This is not so in the case of the corporate takeover. This activity literally burst onto the scene in the mid-1980's as the product of the brilliant mind of Michael Milken, a trader who developed the "junk bond" market that made takeovers on a large scale possible. In just a six year span running from 1982 to 1988, Milken and his band created a movement that launched ten-thousand corporate takeovers, seizing control of enterprises with capital in excess of $1 trillion.[27] The activity created the financial sector's first large group of billionaires, and put corporations on notice that things were about to change.

---

27   Kleinknecht, *The Man Who Sold The World*, p.146.

IN A WORK entitled *The Money Culture*, Michael Lewis has pointed to Bruce Wasserstein as the "patron saint" of the hostile takeover.[28] If this is so, then Michael Milken gets the honor of being the corporate raider's most brilliant missionary, for it was Milken, the extraordinary financial innovator and organizer, who gathered and directed a group of takeover artists with such skill that he became the dominant force in pushing Wall Street from the economy's back burner to the front. Milken's secret was to combine brilliance and ambition with a sense of adventure perhaps never before seen in the financial world.

Born and educated in California, it was as a graduate student that Milken did pioneer work on the corporate bond market. Following his education in the West, he moved East because that's where the real money could be made. He arrived in New York in the 1970's as an unassuming young man who was uncomfortable with the formality of Eastern culture. He considered himself somewhat of an outsider, but nevertheless understood that New York was where he needed to be if he was to become a force in the financial world. So he and his wife settled there, looking like oddities in their breezy California dress until he single-handedly created the junk bond market and used this creation to launch the take-over movement. This feat transformed the outsider into the inside man. By the time Milken was through, paternalistic capitalism was dead, replaced by a new,

28   Lewis, *The Money Culture*, p. xiv.

predatory form where names like Ivan Boesky and Robert Eaton came to define the values of the new era.[29] It took less than a decade for Milken and his cohorts to completely change the way the country did business.

MILKEN'S IDEAS ON the corporate bond market, the key to financing takeovers, germinated early on, when as a young graduate student, he became fascinated with studies that had been done on low rated corporate bonds. He found that when the bonds of poorly performing corporations fell to a B or C rating, it did not necessarily mean that they became a poor investment. On the contrary, Milken found that these "fallen angels" could produce greater returns than their A-rated cousins because their interest rates were higher and their chance of failure was greatly exaggerated. He used this insight when he came to Drexel Burnham Lambert in New York. Here he developed a large group of clients who would buy the cheaply priced bonds he recommended. It was a brand new market that Milken was developing. This market which eventually became known as the "junk bond" market became the mechanism for raising the money that would that would be used to seize control of successful corporations.

---

29   Boesky eventually went to jail for his arbitrage activities, but Eaton, Chrysler's CEO, went on to make $250 million by selling to Dymler Benz the corporation the American public had bailed out only two decades earlier.

IT WAS IN the 1980's that Milken's skills and vision all came together. From the point of view of a modern financial analyst, he saw that the market had seriously undervalued the assets of corporate America. Stock prices were too low, too undervalued, given the profits corporations were making. These low valuations were reflected in the low market activity of that era, and in the deflated dividends that were being paid to shareholders. Corporate board members kept dividends meager in those years because companies appropriated a large percentage of their total revenues to wages, benefits and R&D. To see just how undervalued corporate America was, we need only recall that PE ratios of 30 were considered high in the 70's. The DOW in the 1970's hovered much of the time in the 700's. Compare that to its present 13,000 plus level.

Milken appreciated that corporations were worth much more than their stock prices were indicating. This is what made takeovers so appealing. Companies hung like ripe fruit, waiting to be picked by those with big appetites. What Milken did was use his junk bonds to borrow the money he needed to seize the controlling shares of common stock in various companies. His junk bond creation suddenly made every company in the US vulnerable to a takeover.

MILKEN'S METHOD WAS essentially to recruit the CEO's of rather small corporations to join him in a takeover. He used these companies to raise sizable amounts of money by selling junk bonds in their names in the bond markets he had developed. He then used this money to seize control of much larger corporations. Once in control, corporate boards were forced to focus on short term profits and dividends so stock prices would rise, making the players in the takeover fabulously wealthy.

Here is the step-by-step approach that Milken used to affect these takeovers. First he raised the needed cash by convincing a small corporation to allow him to sell huge amounts of junk bonds under their company's name. With the revenue his bonds raised, he seized control of firms ten times the size of his client firms. A company that was successfully taken this way was then made to issue new bonds in order to pay off the money raised in the original junk bond sale. This of course left the firm that had been seized straddled with debt, one of the reasons it became necessary to squeeze wages and downsize. What better way to pay for the takeover? It even offered the possibility of raising the impression that productivity was rising since the same amount of work was being done by fewer people. Anyone who wished to see what was really happening could easily check the productivity tables, for these show a precipitous drop in the rate of productivity increases when measured by the hour. Productivity rates in the 1950's and 60's were significantly higher than they were in the age of Milken, if they are measured as output/hour. This was especially true in the 80's, before computers made the base cause of productivity increases less clear.

Corporate heads, of course, found that they were in as great a danger of being fired as were their underlings, unless they played ball and declared good dividends. They very quickly learned to adopt the philosophy that worked for them. They focused on the task of becoming rich, synchronizing, as it were, their goals and ethics with those who owned the controlling share of stock in the company they ran. The Providence Journal has noted that according to the *New Yorker* magazine, COE's in 1965 made 20 times more than the typical employee. Now they earn 270 times more.[30] Obviously, a new operating psychology has come to permeate corporate America.

The Small Fries Come To Power

Through Milken, small corporate players were made fabulously wealthy, and became his devoted followers. They saw that this was a man whose genius and ambition could make them kings. In *The Predator's Ball,* Connie Bruck quotes a guest at the annual party Milken liked to throw as saying that on this particular night, "Milken was more wired than ever," preaching the messianic message that, "they all needed 'to save corporate America from itself.'"[31] Milken often vocalized the view that his takeovers were making

---

30   See Bill Reynolds, *The Providence Journal,* October 26, 2013.

31   Connie Bruck, *The Predator's Ball: The Inside Story of Drexel Burnham and The Rise Of The Junk Bond Raiders.* Penguin Books. New York, 1989. see especially pp.13-16.

corporate America more efficient. Remarkably, they still make this claim. But it's doubtful that Milken ever really believed that the world's most powerful economy and its most plentiful society was actually bloated and sclerotic, as he accused it of being. He and the corporate raiders he launched have always advertised themselves as the country's benifactors.

A PRIME EXAMPLE of the raiders rather sanguine view of what they were doing was T. Boone Pickens. Pickens, who currently dispenses his advice on what US energy policy should be, boasted in 1985 that 750,000 stockholders had been able to scoop up $13 billion, thanks to his raids on four big oil companies in just two years. "I am," he declared, "the champion of the small stockholder,"[32] a fact that although somewhat true, brought little comfort to those American workers who paid the price for all of this. For that $13 billion in dividends was paid for by downsizing, squeezing wages, and cheapening products.

Pickens, like all of the other raiders, first secured his fortune and then claimed to be enriching us all. It's a satisfying mental feat that the raiders love to take comfort in. Victor Icahn still occasionally graces the pages of the Wall Street Journal's op-ed page, arguing that mergers and acquisitions bring needed efficiency to our enterprises, especially in a global economy. How strange then that so few other nations have bought into this. Germany, for example, will

---

32   "*The Raider,.*" Business Wee*k*, March 4, 1985, p.80.

not allow their companies to be taken. They prevent it by employing laws referred to as "poison pills."[33] A Wall Street Journal headline which read "Japan's Companies Gird For Attack"[34] also sums up the foreign attitude. Countries outside of the English speaking world have never accepted the efficiency argument. B. Mark Smith, commenting on the European fear of America's raider culture notes,

> The traditional social compacts- often
> referred to as stakeholder capitalism,
> where labor, creditors, local communities,
> and governments have an important voice
> in corporate decision making- are
> jeopardized by the new found power
> of stock market investors who demand
> that management concentrate first and
> foremost on maximizing profits and
> dividends.[35]

The former secretary of the UK Takeover Panel, dismayed by European resistance to takeovers complained that, "The message is that it is fortress Europe, and that European countries should be protected

---

33   Smith, B. Mark, *The Equity Culture, The Equity Culture, The Story of the Global Stock Market.*, New York, Farrar, Straus and Giroux, 2003. p. 290.
34   *"Japan's Companies Gird For Attack"* Wall Street Journal, April 30, 2008, p. A4
35   Smith, *The Equity Culture*, p. 289.

from overseas predators."[36] His criticism is actually an accurate summary. Gerhard Schroeder, the former German Chancellor who reformed the German welfare system, viewed the American financial sector as predatory as he set down the European opposition to the US's obsessed takeover sector with the statement, "Don't count on me to Americanize German society.[37]

By and large, the difference in our acceptance of mergers and acquisitions and Europe's rejection of them rests on the fact that the US and UK have always been more friendly to the idea of unfettered markets. This became especially true during the Reagan-Thatcher revolution, when a new generation of lawyers and economists, whose views were much more free-market oriented than those of their predecessors, took over the anti-trust division of the Justice Department. As soon as the new group stepped in, they issued guidelines superseding those that had been passed in the 1960's. These guidelines indicated that government would take a much more lenient view towards mergers than it had in the past.[38] Milken must have grinned at this statement of innocence.

Without controls, the simple truth is that mergers and acquisitions are too lucrative for the financial sector to resist. Milken's original conception is so elegant in its simplicity, making so much money so easily

---

36   Ibid., 293.

37   Ibid.

38   John Ehrman, *The Eighties: America in the Age of Reagan*, New Haven, Yale University Press, pp. 96-97.

that it's no wonder the raiders came to attach themselves to it. Their newly found methods allowed them to stride through the American economy and make themselves billionaires as they wreaked their havoc on the middle class. Unsuspectingly, we all accepted their revolution. Many, in fact, welcomed it. Laissez Faire philosophy in the 1980's was in the air, and would continue unabated during the Clinton years.

BESIDES PICKENS AND Icahn, there were a host of young players who joined the acquisition game with a boldness that could only be found in the young. There was Saul Steinberg, who at age 27 made his bid to buy Chemical Bank. Steinberg soon went on to pick a fight with Disney, perhaps motivated by both childhood nostalgia as well as by the lure of money. And then there was oil baron Marvin Davis of Denver who bought Twentieth Century Fox, and then pulled $539 million out of it to pay for some of the debt he had taken on by buying it. Fox was then forced to raise an estimated $400 million to pay for its new debt. It also had to cancel production on a number of scheduled movies.[39] William Farley, another takeover artist who was hardly a big name at the time, noted that when he started in 1976, "no one was really geared up to finance this stuff. Today(1985), we could go out and probably raise $1 billion in two days."[40] Indeed Drexel, Milken's home base, had learned important lessons

39   Bruck, *The Predators Ball.*

40   *Business Week*, p. 84

from their employee and raised $1.5 billion for Icahn in a tension filled few days in February, 1985.

The 1980's was the decade that the takeover fever grew red hot. At his ball, Milken's men, this "band of mainly small time entrepreneurs,"[41] who had all used their companies to raise takeover money, had become transformed overnight. Very quickly, "this band", who were "the have-nots of the corporate world", became the new force in the US economy.[42] While addressing his group, Milken told them that they represented a combined buying power of three trillion dollars,[43] all to be directed at every conceivable type of industry. Banks, chemical companies, retail chains, everything was a target. Within a little over a decade, Milken had acquired the ability to transform corporate behavior in a way that punished everyone except those who were in on the deal. It wouldn't be too long afterward that this type of activity was taken over by firms that actually looked respectable, firms that we would come to call Private Equity (PE) firms.. But it was the junk bond traders who originally changed the face of corporate America. The member's of Milken's tribe, who sometimes needed to be reassured, felt comforted by Milken's Messianic claim that he was transforming the American economy, restructuring it so that it could operate as a more efficient machine. To see this claim for what it was one need only turn to Milken's

---

41   Bruck, *The Predator's Ball*, p. 20.

42   Ibid.

43   Bruck, *The Preditor's Ball*, p. 13.

relationship with Ivan Boesky, who Milken partnered up with in 1985. Together, Milken and Boesky carried out the largest arbitrage capitalization in history.[44] Boesky, driven by his dream to be the next Rothschild, raised 220 million dollars while Milken raised 600 million. Since they could leverage this sum at three to one, Milken effectively set Boesky loose with two and one half billion dollars to terrorize the big corporations of America. As Milken told him, "we're going to tee-up GM, Ford, and IBM . . . and make them cringe."[45] And cringe they did. It was in these years that General Motors ceased being called "Generous Motors." The old style of paternalism had come to an end.[46]

As time progressed, the quest for easy riches made financiers less patient. At Drexel, they learned to set up dummy companies on paper, and then issue bundles of junk bonds in their name. With the revenue it raised, Drexel gained control of firms through a tender offer. And as their creativity and imagination continued to lead to new possibilities, their stranglehold on corporate America continued to grow. Leveraged buyouts (LBO's) became and remain a major focus of Wall Street activity.

Then and Now - The Fruits of Milken's Labor

Despite the claims that the raiders have all made, claiming they were fostering American efficiency,

44   Ibid. p.200

45   Ibid., p. 94

46   Paul Krugman, *The Great Unraveling,* New York: W.W.Norton, 2005

everything about the way they operated points to the opposite conclusion. One of Milken's dark secrets was the fact that he was privy to the knowledge that there was, and remains, a tendency for many of the firms that are raided to go bankrupt. This was as true then as it is now with the PE firms that have institutionalized the corporate takeover. Since takeovers are financed by the acquisition of huge debt, they oftentimes cause firms to totter on the brink once they are seized. Milken saw this danger and cleverly disguised the problem by usually having his raiders borrow more than was needed. This allowed extra cash to service the acquired debt for at least a couple of years. If the firm then did collapse, enough time had elapsed to shift blame to other issues.[47]

Despite declarations to the contrary, in the post-Milken world, much of what occurs is simply theft, practiced on corporations that are plunged into debt, and practiced on the American people who, as a group, continue to pay a steep price for this activity. Yes, it's true that such theft has always been a part of capitalism, but theft on this scale, and with the boldness of Milken and his raiders, is new. When Ivan Boesky declared at a college commencement that "greed is good" it was such a shocking break with our cultural values that Oliver Stone seized upon the declaration to fashion a classic American villain, Gordon Gecko. In Gecko, we see

---

47   Joseph Stiglitz, *The Roaring Nineties*, New York, W. W. Norton, 2003. p. 273. See also Alan J. Auerbach, ed. *Causes and Consequences*. Chicago: Univ. of Chicago Press, 1988.

greed so twist the human spirit that all we are left with is a stunted individual, fabulously rich, but still nothing more than a moral dumbbell. His negatives make him unforgettable, and leave us to ponder how many more like him there are out there, leading and directing the charge of the system that has spawned them.

Oliver Stone is not alone. Taking up this subject of larceny, Joseph Stiglitz, a noted Nobel Prize winning economist, has no problem seeing Wall Street's activities as simple thievery. He notes that the 1990's was the decade that saw the perfection of the skills that were required for "hidden thievery" on a scale never witnessed before.[48] Even worse, the years that followed Milken's work saw corporate CEO's rewarded with riches "beyond the dreams of all but the cleverest of the manipulators of the seventies and early eighties."[49]

Charles Gasparino, who covers Wall street for a major TV network, has noted the same thing. By the 1990's, he says, stockbrokers no longer had an interest in recommending safe, long term investments.

> They made their fortunes by churning the accounts of their customers, essentially trading shares they didn't need in order to generate commissions. Bankers didn't buy their second home in the Hamptons simply by telling a company how to manage its cash flow; the trick was to get the typical CEO

---

48   Stiglitz, *The Roaring 90's*, p.273.
49   Ibid.

in the 1980's to grow a company by acquisitions, often using debt to finance the deal.[50]

John Kenneth Galbraith notes in his *New Industrial State* that if you were a fly on the wall of a corporate boardroom in 1965, you would have seen a group of managers apportioning a small part of their company's profits to a small and "insignificant" group of shareholders. You'd also be aware of the fact that CEO salaries were not excessively large.

> Indeed, by modern standards, . . . [they]were tiny compared to today's lavish packages. Executives didn't focus single-mindedly on maximizing stock prices; they thought of themselves as serving multiple constituencies, including their employees. The quintessential . . . corporation was known internally as Generous Motors.[51]

If you now fast forward to a boardroom in our present era, you'll see a much more aggressive group, nervously analyzing quarterly profits and earnings/

---

50   Charles Gasparino, *The Sellout: How Three Decades of Wall Street Greed and Government Mismanagement Destroyed the Global financial System.* New York, Harper Collins, 2009, p16.

51   Krugman, *The Great Unraveling,* pp.110

share, making sure that they meet the projections that the financial sector has made. The unease these executives feel is based on the sure knowledge that disappointing Wall Street can mean getting downsized, renovated, or whatever else we wish to call "getting fired".

The postwar era of the late 1940's, 50's, and 60's, was an era where corporate executives controlled their own boardrooms, and made their decisions on the basis of what was best for their corporate organization. Today, this power of control is gone. All decisions must be made with an eye on the reaction of "The Street." Board members all understand that their survival depends upon it. In a very interesting book on the evolution of our ideas on the market, Justin Fox points out that it didn't take long for CEO's to see the new way the game was being played. In Fox's words, after Wall Street gained control of corporate decision making,

> "They [CEO's] had ceased to be kings."
> Many of them reacted to their new status
> entirely rationally . . . by ditching
> noblesse oblige and becoming dictators,
> aware that they might be deposed in a
> putsch at any moment. They grabbed as
> much treasure as possible before that
> happened."[52]

---

52   Fox, *The Myth of the Rational Market*, p. 274.

This whole new reality, pioneered by Milken and brought to maturity by present-day PE (private equity) firms, rests on a strange new way of viewing corporate responsibility.

In a view peculiar only to the US, and perhaps to the UK as well, corporate responsibility is thought to be completely divorced from the well being of the society they function in. In this model, corporations exist solely for the purpose of making money for their shareholders. That they occupy space in the US, use a labor force that has been educated by the taxpayer, and use infrastructure that is built and maintained by taxes means nothing. That we are all members of the same society means nothing. That they have a responsibility for helping to maintain the quality of that society also means nothing. This is Ayan Rand's dream world. It is a world completely devoid of any recognition of the fact that all market transactions, including those between employer and employee, must be mutually beneficial if the system is to succeed in the long run. The American free-market system has been hijacked by one of its appendages. Through various means, finance has been able to claim portions of corporate wealth that it has done nothing to earn.

In essence, an economy that was once directed by relatively modest corporate technocrats who kept their eye on long-term prosperity has fallen into the hands of a new breed of bankers and traders who expect and demand corporate board members to do their bidding. The degree to which this new group has succeeded is the degree to which the fortunes of the middle class have declined.

The Magnitude Of The Change

Is it possible to calculate the overall toll the merger and acquisition movement has taken on American workers? Kleinknect, in *The Man Who Sold the World,* suggests we multiply the three hundred "redundant" workers that were downsized in the Bendix take-over by hundreds of thousands.[53] If we do, it pushes downsized workers into the hundred million range, a figure that's roughly two-thirds of the American labor force.[54] If Kleinknect's estimates are even close to being true, imagine the instability that has been introduced into people's lives by takeovers.   It's an interesting number to muse over.

Kevin Phillips, a respected commentator on economic subjects, has explained how the bankers have gotten away with all this. "Over the last three decades," Phillips notes, "finance cannily sidestepped the spotlight" suggesting that US finance occupied "some small periphery of the US economy."[55] But in fact, starting in the 80's, the financial sector grew, until by 2007, the people in charge had become the "Masters and Mistresses of the universe."[56]

---

53   Kleinknecht, *The Man Who Sold the World,* p. 151
54   Ibid.
55   Phillips, *Bad Money.* P. 48
56   Ibid..

To get the full flavor of the magnitude of Milken's transformation, one need only to look at the growth of debt in the US financial sector. In 1979, its total outstanding debt was $505 billion. By 1989 it had jumped to $2.4 trillion and by 1999, it stood at 7.6 trillion. By 2006 the 7.6 figure had doubled again,[57] to a figure thirty times larger than it was in 1979. Much of this debt was acquired to pay for hostile takeovers. Here is the triumph of the leveraged buyout.

Today, the PE firms who continue this work have learned to operate on a scale that not even Milken could have imagined. Our corporations now borrow to refinance their debt. In the past, they carried hardly any debt, and when they did, it was to build plants. Add another worry to the problems the US economy is now beset with.

In 2008, The Boston Consulting Group estimated that approximately 50% of all PE owned companies are in danger of default. [58] This is a telling statement on what the real effects of the mergers and acquisitions movement has been. It's only beneficiaries have been the big banks, the Private Equity firms, and the lawyers who do the legal work.

$

---

57   Ibid p.44

58   Kosman, The Buyout of America, p. 8.

Chapter 3.
Securitization - How Wall Street Cost Millions of People Their Jobs

None of this makes sense, I thought...
why a near global stock market meltdown
. . .simply because of some mortgage
foreclosures? After all, the problem
loans amounted to, at worst, $200 billion
in a global market worth hundreds of
trillions.
David Smick, *The World is Curved*

Similarities- The US and Ireland

The Republic of Ireland is a small country with an economy roughly the size of the state of Maryland's. Yet, despite its size, it serves as an interesting point of study because in recent years its economic history has paralleled that of our own in two very significant ways.

First, the Irish economy achieved remarkable growth by rapidly expanding its high tech sector. Then, the nation experienced an economic collapse on so large a scale that it presently threatens the stability of the entire Euro Zone. In a simplified way, this is all reminiscent of what happened here in the US.

Ireland's fall, like our own, was not caused, as recessions usually are, by a contraction in consumer spending. Here lies the second way in which the Irish experience resembles the American. Not only did the small nation grow for the same reasons that we did, it also suffered an economic collapse for the same reasons. The crash of the Irish economy was precipitated by irresponsible banking practices on a scale perhaps never witnessed before in the nation's history. The full story of this fall is only now beginning to emerge.

IN THE MID 1990's, after the US had revolutionized the computer and telecommunications industries, American firms began to look for new lands to expand to. Quickly, Ireland turned up in their sights as a major area worth looking at, and eventually it experienced a large influx of high tech firms. The movement of American technology into Ireland pulled the small nation out of the economic doldrums and placed it at the head of the EU (European Union) nations.

The specifics of Ireland's race to the economic summit began in 1995, when Intel made the momentous decision to move some of their operations to County Kildare.[59] Because of Intel's prestigious reputation, their decision sent vibrations throughout the

---

59   Fintan O'Toole, *Ship of Fools: How Stupidity and Corruption Sank the Celtic Tiger,* Public Affairs, Perseus Book Group, 2010, p14.

high tech industry, signaling other American firms that Ireland was a place to be. The pull became so strong that pharmaceuticals soon followed: Pfizer, which opened facilities in County Cork, began manufacturing all of its Viagra there.[60]

Outsourcing from the US to Ireland grew at such a rapid pace that by 2000, Ireland had $38,000 worth of foreign investment for every man, woman, and child, a figure representing more than six times the EU average. In just five years, American firms came to account for more than half of all Irish manufacturing, raising the nation's per capita GDP from what in 1991 was 75% of the EU average to an eye-popping 111% by 1999.

This was the kind of success that economists dream of, because it was built by increasing the productive output of the Irish people. It was tangible, job creating growth, unlike the type that results from inflating real estate prices or speculative bank loans.

After its economy surged, what happened next was a portent of what would soon happen in the US. Buoyed by the country's new wealth, Irish banks began to indulge in reckless real estate loans. Rising wages from the tech boom led to an expanding mortgage market, whetting the appetites of financiers. Soon, banks began taking bigger and bigger risks as they continually sought bigger returns. Gambling in real estate came to take on a life of its own.[61] Prices

---

60   Ibid.

61   See especially, David J.Lynch, *When The Luck Of The Irish Ran Out,* Palgrave Macmillan, 2010.

pushed to dizzying heights, racing past what the nation's wage structure could support.[62] The bubble burst in 2005, two years before our own did, leaving the Irish people helplessly looking on as prices fell. With the fall, banks became insolvent, loans stopped, and the economy collapsed.

To this now familiar scenario was added another story, also familiar to Americans. The Irish government, encouraged by the eat-drink-and-be-merry atmosphere of the 1990's, became addicted to profligate spending.[63] When the boom ended, it found itself with falling tax revenues and rising debts. To meet these responsibilities, the government sold more bonds, raising the Irish debt load so high that investors, fearing a government default, began selling off these bonds. It was this sell-off that threatened the stability of the entire Euro Zone.[64]

It's become a familiar story. Banks, whose job it is to connect those who have capital with those who don't have ceased operating simply as a conduit for money. They've developed an appetite for sums that cannot be made if they simply stick to their primary purpose. In Ireland, and even more so in the US, banks have become the defining economic force of the nation, exercising power well beyond the services they were designed to provide.

---

62   O'Toole, *Ship Of Fools.*, pp 23-24.

63   Ibid. passim

64   The problem of instability jumping from one country to another is the subject of the next chapter..

For Americans, the value of the Irish experience lies in the gift of clarity that it offers. Lacking the confusing complexities of the American landscape, Ireland's recent history gives us an overview of exactly what it was that happened here, as our own economy unraveled, step by step.

Summarizing The American Experience

During the last five years of the Clinton Administration, the American economy had become the eighth wonder of the world. Its young entrepreneurs, who in the 90's were still just entering early middle age, had single-handedly created a world of technological wonders. Our economic job growth was envied everywhere. Taxes poured into the government's coffers in such amounts that the nation ran a budget surplus in Clinton's last year in office. Our confidence in the economy had reached unparalleled heights, causing many economists to insist that we were no longer susceptible to the swings of the business cycle. Then the "dot com" bubble burst. This was the opening shot across the bow, warning that Wall Street's speculation, fed by the money the Fed was making available to banks, was taking tech stocks to unsustainable heights. All the rules on the price to earning ratios of these stocks were broken. In the 1970's, PE's of twenty five were considered high.[65] In the 90's, tech stocks routinely had PE's in

---

65   As the name implies, PE's are derived by dividing the price of a stock by its earnings per share.

the hundreds. Some were actually in the thousands, and we were still reassured, being told that tech stocks were not subject to the rules of ordinary stocks. They were. Shortly after the "dot com" bubble burst, the scandals at Enron and World.Com served to reinforce an emerging recognition of the fact that a new way of doing business now engulfed Wall Street.

The process of dangerous speculation continued in the Bush years when the Congress, with its newly discovered ally, the banks, found a new investment area to inflate. Fannie-Mae and Freddie Mac, aided by the dramatic loosening of lending rules that had occurred under Clinton, helped precipitate a housing bubble that began expanding in the early years of the 21st. century. It finally burst in 2007, when it helped bring down the entire world economy.

Washington and New York, operating as partners in the housing market, had gambled and lost. The entire global banking system froze up and a world wide recession followed. With a sudden quickness, reminiscent of Ireland, everything unraveled. The recession cut so deeply that the only people to escape an interruption in their income flow were the very same people who had caused the problem, the "bankers". The government saved them by offering the taxpayers the argument (perhaps justifiable) that the banks had become too big to fail.

Some knew that what had been going on could not be sustained,[66] although not many expected the

66   David Smick, *The World Is Curve: Hidden Dangers To the Global Economy*, New York: Penguin Group, 2009, Preface.

correction to drag down the entire global economy. As David Smick noted, how could a $200 billion mortgage market pull down a global market worth hundreds of trillions? It would take some time before the details of Wall Street's machinations became more generally known, providing the answer to this puzzling question.

This chapter will discuss how it came to be that a limited mortgage market was able to take down the entire financial system of the developed world, and cost Americans the loss of at least six million jobs. It's a story filled with the ingenuity that only inordinate greed could inspire.

To understand how all of this happened, we need to go back to the 1980's, to the same period when Milken and his raiders began putting their own particular squeeze on the American worker.

WHEN THE DECADE of the 80's began, being an investment banker was a good business to be in, but not one that would usually make you rich. Your job essentially was to advise corporate clients on what to fill their portfolios with.

In those now distant days, the financial sector earned only a small fraction of the nation's total corporate profits. By the end of George W. Bush's first term, however, this figure, as we've noted, had reached 48%,[67] an astounding percentage considering the fact that the banking system is nothing more than

---

67   Phillips, *Bad Money*, p. 34.

a transfer station for money. It's obviously an important service, but why the rewards should be nearly 50% of all corporate profits remains a question that needs to be raised.

In 2010, the Goldman Sachs Group paid its thirty six thousand employees eight billion dollars in salaries, a figure that averages out to $300,000 per worker.[68] This is six times the average American family income, yet even it is dwarfed by the income paid out by many of New York's hedge funds. Meanwhile, the economic collapse that these institutions precipitated have led to dramatic unemployment and underemployment throughout the nation.

Seeking to revive our damaged economy, the government has spent $862 billion on a stimulus, while the Fed has helped to feed a new stock market bubble by spending approximately $1.25 trillion, buying up the bad mortgage securities that had earned the banks billions in profits when they were originally sold.[69] To these two historic bailout programs we have to add an additional $900 billion which was raised by the sale of long term Treasuries. The total cost of all of this bailout and stimulus activity is $3.5 trillion, a figure so large that the government, if it had chose to, could have mailed every American family approximately $45,000.

Nor does it end here. There is a hidden cost as well, a cost the numbers can't include. In an economy

68   *Wall Street Journal,* January 28, 2011, p. 1.
69   Ibid.

that is fueled by so much speculation, a lot of capital is diverted away from the productive uses it otherwise would have been directed to. Banks diverted $trillions of seed money that could have been used for solid investment in business to avenues of activity created by banks for the exclusive profit and benefit of banks.[70]

Like Ireland, the false perception of prosperity that bank activity created gave government an excuse to spend at levels that now threaten to

> crush our children, constrict the
> economy in which they operate, make
> America poorer, lower its standing
> in the world, and do in the American
> dream.[71]

All of this raises the question: How did banks ever become large enough to precipitate such a catastrophe? A case can be made for the claim that the care-free gambling psychology of the financial sector, encouraged by the libertarian leadership of financiers like Alan Greenspan, Robert Rubin and Larry Summers, transferred itself to Washington as it linked arms with Wall Street in areas like deregulation, mortgages and bailouts that served the interests of the people who

---

70   For an excellent discussion of this misallocation of capital see *"The Great Misallocators"*, The Wall Street Journal, January 26, 2011, p. A18

71   Peggy Noonan, *"An Unserious Speech Misses The Mark"*, The Wall Street Journal, January 29-30, 2011, p. A17

gave us the crises rather than the direct interests of the general public. Congressman Barney Frank, as we will point out, was so taken by the spirit of those years that he even used the gamblers vocabulary in describing Congress' actions when he argued that the sub-prime mortgage loans, although risky, were "worth the roll of the dice." Like the Irish, we went from stable technological growth, with a budget that was balanced, to a form of speculative finance that encouraged government to spend and subsidize recklessly until it resulted in a doubling of the size of the Federal government in just ten years.[72] How did our banking system, and our government get so out of control?

The Dizzying Account Of What Wall Street Banks Did

Like so many of the changes our nation has undergone, the growth of the financial sector to its present gargantuan size has its roots in the demographic anomalies caused by WWII. It was the boomers, moving into adulthood that gave Wall Street an opportunity it couldn't refuse.

By the 1970's, this large demographic group, born during and after WWII, was beginning to move into the housing market, a fact Wall Street recognized but which, as yet, it had not found a way to profit from. The problem would not be solved for another decade, but once it was, it would open the floodgates to the creation of securities that were as ingenious and dangerous as they were profitable. A whole new system,

72   Ibid.

where small (commercial) banks sell mortgages, car loans and the like to large investment banks which then roll them into huge interest paying securities is what emerged once Wall Street figured things out.

THE ENTIRE STORY began at Solomon Brothers where, in the mid-1980's, investment banker Lewis Ranieri was pondering the problem of how home mortgages could be bought and sold as a bond. Called the "Godfather" of the mortgage bond,[73] Ranieri was tantalized by the steady stream of mortgage revenue that Americans were famous for faithfully paying, but which Wall Street could not get its hands on. With the exception of a small number of Federal mortgage bonds that were put up for sale in the 1970's by Ginnie Mae, mortgages simply were not traded. The small commercial banks that wrote them held onto them.[74]

This all began to change in 1977, when John Gutfreund, the CEO at Solomon's, called Ranieri into his office and told him that the movement of the "boomers" into the housing market was simply too big to allow these mortgages to be held onto by small banks. There was a fortune to be made trading them if a way could be found to turn them into a large security. Ranieri was ordered to find a way to trade the avalanche that was soon to arrive. It was Gutfreund's belief that this high school dropout, who had started in the mail room at $70/week, had the drive and the

73   Gasparino, *The Sellout1*, p.xiii.

74   Ibid., p. 19.

creative juices to get the job done. Ranieri wasn't so sure. There was no investment interest in a mortgage bond. Who would buy them? He feared he was being assigned to a financial backwater.

One of the problems Ranieri faced was the fact that commercial banks were not allowed to remove mortgages from their balance sheets. The mortgages that they wrote were their own obligation, so each bank was limited in what they could write by the amount of capital they possessed. Very importantly, this limited the number of bonds that mortgages could be rolled into. Not until late into the Clinton era was this obstacle removed.

As expected, things took a while to get started. It was a new market Ranieri was developing and there was confusion over the bonds he was writing. Were they being issued by a bank or by some underwriter? Only gradually did Ranieri himself become a believer in them, and that only after he turned to government and hired a team of lobbyists to secure tax advantages for S&L's selling mortgages. This stimulated the mortgage market and allowed him to take advantage of the rising bond market as he converted as many of these mortgages into securities as the law would allow. He was off and running as the bond market began to explode.[75]

Ranieri started pooling mortgages into bonds called Residential Mortgage Backed Securities (RMBS). As his success spread, others noticed. In particular, Lawrence Fink at First Boston noticed.[76]

---

75   Ibid.

76   Ibid., p.23

It was now 1983 and Larry Fink was struck by the idea that Ranieri's RMBS's could be divided into different levels of risk, levels that came to be referred to as "tranches". Tranches that brought the highest level of risk would, of course, bring the highest return. These mortgage tranches became known as Collateralized Mortgage Obligations or CMO's.[77] Fink's CMO's were the first real sign of what was coming.

With his CMO's, Fink became a Wall Street rock star.[78] Soon he found ways to combine tranches from particular CMO's with tranches from other CMO's.[79] Eventually, this process of combining tranches of different asset backed securities produced "a highly heterogeneous mix of debt securities"[80] that now go by the name of Collateralized Debt Obligations or CDO's.

As time passed, CDO's became mesmerizingly complex because they combined tranches from one type of pool, such as auto loans, with tranches from other types of pools, such as mortgage pools, student loan pools, credit card pools, and the like. Every conceivable type of consumer loan payment was made into a vehicle for profit.

As these expanding levels of securitization increased, the danger of no longer knowing what

---

77   Ibid.

78   Ibid., p. 24.

79   Kenneth Scott and John Taylor, *Wall Street Journal,* "Why Toxic Assets Are So Hard to Clean Up", July, 2009.

80   Ibid.

the real value of these CDO's were was increasing dramatically. It was rapidly becoming impossible for banks to calculate what it was that they were buying and selling. But the dangers associated with this loss of transparency seemed, at the time, irrelevant. Everyone who needed reassurance was able to take comfort in the fact that these CDO's were structured on brilliant probability models that small groups of mathematicians had developed. So secure did these models seem that banks eventually unveiled the ultimate security, the CDO squared, then the penultimate CDO cubed. These securities were so complex that if you owned a CDO squared that held corporate loans which had been pooled into 100 Collateralized Loan Obligations or CLO's, each of which held 250 corporate loans, you would need information on 25,000 underlying loans to determine the true value of your security. And should your CDO squared hold 100 CDO's, each of which held 100 RMBS' made up of only 2,000 mortgages, you would need information on 20 million underlying loans to clearly see what the underlying value of each security was.[81]

This lack of transparency is at the heart of the reasons why bank loans have seized up and haven't yet moved back to normal levels, despite the trillions of dollars of bailout money that governments around the world have poured into their vaults. Banks continue to hold trillions of dollars in securities whose

81   Ibid.

true value can only be guessed at. David Smick has summarized the crises this way.

> At the heart of the great credit crises of 2007-2008 was nothing less than a crises of trust in financial architecture.[82]

Brewing more deeply than the bursting housing bubble and subprime problem was;

> the widespread, worldwide distrust of the asset backed securities market.[83]
> All of the securitized products that Wall Street had written had come to;
> represent a central artery in the global economy's bloodstream for credit allocation. The subprime crises triggered the clogging of that artery due to a lack of confidence and trust.[84]

The global recession took place because credit dried up everywhere. Global bankers would no longer buy the asset backed securities that had become their collateral. Much of the world's vital capital had been wasted on flim-flam paper products instead of going into corporate loans. "The central artery . . . for credit", asset-backed securities could not be verified since they lacked transparency. And when we consider the fact that institutions borrow against their

---

82   Smick, *The World is Curved.*, *p. 249.*

83   Ibid.

84   Ibid.

current assets to make new investments (a process referred to as leveraging) the problem of loans freezing up became even greater. A financial train wreck occurred because all of the buyers of asset backed securities, among which were pension funds, insurance companies, trusts, foreign banks and hedge funds- all found themselves holding down-graded securities that no one would buy. The backbone of the financial system could no longer serve as collateral.[85]

Deregulating The Banks Changed Everything

In theory, pooling large numbers of mortgages greatly reduces the risks of mortgages failing through homeowner default because the mortgage securities contain so many sound mortgages that the ones that default can be absorbed by the large numbers that don't. By spreading the risk, Ranieri's mortgage bond creations seemed to provide a service to the economy, but only if sold in moderation. As we now know, these securities were quickly recognized to be a potentially easy ticket to enormous profits, and so there was no resistance to selling too many of them. They allowed for very big and quick commissions. This is what led to the complex CDO's that had sliced mortgage bonds into tranches and then added a bewildering array of other types of consumer loans. In time their value came to dwarf the subprime mortgages that triggered their demise.

---

85   Ibid., p. 250.

WHEN RANIERI'S ASSET backed securities were first released, commercial banks, those banks which write our mortgages and issue our checking accounts were still limited in the number of mortgages they could originate. Their loans, by law, could not exceed their assets, so their sale to Wall Street was still restricted. As yet, Gutfreund's dream was unrealized. Stodgy old rules were limiting the sale of mortgages. But he was right. There were huge profits lurking out there if only the rules could be changed.

It was 1997 that became Gutfreund's year. In that year, finance in the US took a quantum leap when President Clinton's administration passed the Financial Services Modernization Act. The new law finally removed the banking restrictions that had tied things up for so long by removing the separation between commercial banking and investment banking, a separation that had been in existence since the 1930's. From New York's point of view, commercial banks needed to be exempted from the strictures that had prevented them from writing an unlimited number of mortgages. They had to remove the requirement that limited mortgage writing to the amount of money banks had in their vaults. They needed to be allowed to sell their mortgages to investment banks. That way, they could write a mortgage, sell it immediately to New York, get their commission, and just keep writing. This is why many commercial banks at the height of the bubble began giving mortgages without even asking for written proof of what a client's income was. They even ignored requiring a statement of proof that the borrower had a job. They were going to sell the mortgage anyway. The Financial Services Modernization Act had handed mortgage originators a perpetual money machine with seemingly no risk. And for a while the system did work, and people made a lot of money. Everything was safe so long as the people getting these mortgages paid their monthly payments. Should a large number of defaults set in, however, panic selling would follow and the banks holding the mortgage bonds would be trapped with paper no one wanted. This is Smick's $200 billion mortgage market. If it was the only danger, it would have been easily absorbed with little more than a slight market indigestion. The problem was all those CDO's. Trillions of dollars' worth. They are what magnified the problem because they were subject to panic selling if the mortgage market triggered a stampede. Of course, this is exactly what it did. Some hedge funds saw it coming. They sold their asset-backed securities and then sold their bank stocks short, adding to the $billions they had made in the run up. But most big banks got caught. This ending was all too clear for those who wanted to see it. That the high risk mortgages the government had encouraged would be paid steadily on a monthly schedule was an illusion, but most really did not want to ponder this obvious fact. Too much quick money was being made.

WHILE IT'S USUALLY true that old habits die hard, it didn't take long for the banks to lose all restraint in mortgage writing, as we've seen. All of the careful lending practices of the past disappeared as scrutiny by small banks went out the window and as large banks were now given a free hand to enter the fray. As Charles Gasperino has noted,

> Among the vast changes it [the 1997 law] allowed was the ability of these new financial behemoths like Citigroup to combine commercial and investment bank operations under one roof, transferring once staid commercial banks into gambling dens of trading increasingly exotic bonds.[86]

Washington could have pinched the housing bubble once it began because they were guaranteeing many of these mortgages through Fannie Mae and Freddie Mack, but they were not of a mind to do so. Instead, they decided to join the party. Through Fannie and Freddie, the Federal government saw a way to get commercial banks to loan to people who were huge credit risks. These loans, known as sub-prime loans, had become of increasing interest to the government because since the 1970's, the working middle class had found it increasingly difficult to enter the housing market. Houses, which in the 1950's and 60's were easy to buy had, by the late 1990's, moved out of the reach of many of the people who, at an earlier time could have afforded them. By

---

86   Gasparino, *The Sellout*, p.196-197.

the turn of the century, housing across the nation had outpaced average inflation by a factor of at least two times. This made the government much more receptive to the idea of guaranteeing risky loans. And the investment banks were certainly more than willing to securitize these loans, since Fannie and Freddie guaranteed them. There was nothing for the banks to lose. Commercial banks could make all the mortgage loans they wished because New York would buy them and New York showed no restraint because if huge numbers of the mortgages they were buying failed, the quasi government insurance companies, Fannie and Freddie would pay off the debt.

By 2004, a single large investment bank owned a billion dollar mortgage pool composed of approximately 7,000 mortgage loans, 90% of which were high risk(sub-prime). Commercial banks, Wall Street investment banks, and Washington had all become collaborators, tied tightly together in a financial partnership that allowed each to feed off the other and serve their distinctive needs. As we've mentioned, Congressman Barney Frank, Chairman of the House Financial Services Committee, announced that he wanted to "roll the dice" on sub-prime mortgages,[87] and give an expanded number of people the ability to enter the housing market. The low interest rates that the Fed established combined with the demand these policies stimulated to produce the housing bubble

87   Peter Wallison, "The Price of Fannie and Freddie Keeps Going Up", WSJ, December 30, 2009.

that eventually triggered the near total collapse of the entire global financial system. It was Ireland all over again, only raised to the tenth power.

On The Question Of Culpability

That the sub-prime market was indeed the trigger that led to the global recession is beyond dispute. And for that Washington bears responsibility. But the financial avalanche that followed the subprime meltdown had roots that run far deeper. On the subject of culpability, David Smick, a man closely associated with the financial markets, and one who certainly could not be accused of having

leftward leanings, writes, as we have quoted in the introduction to this chapter, that the loss of $200 billion, which the sub-prime loans represented, should have caused no more than a ripple in a market worth hundreds of trillions.[88] Under normal conditions, the global marketplace would have cleansed itself rather quickly. It didn't because securitized mortgage bonds had evolved into a mind boggling maze that even to this day, very few people understand.[89] New securities, derived from and incorporating older securities became so staggeringly large that the loans they incorporated became completely opaque. Holders of asset backed securities were unable to determine

88   Smick, *The World Is Curved*,, p. 244.

89   Smick estimates that probably no more than 500 people in the entire world understand the complex securities that banks trade.

whether or not the ones they held incorporated the failed sub-prime loans. That's why $billions in mortgages ruined $trillions worth of securities. In addition, as financiers tried to work their way through the problem, it became increasingly apparent that the value of the paper that had been sold was far in excess of the value of the property they were originally written on. With these securities now selling in the trillions of dollars, the financial world found itself on a tightrope hovering over a canyon. The ingredients for an international collapse had been added to a mix that no one was capable of analyzing. We are all familiar now with the collapse that followed. The conclusion that Wall Street bares the blame is inescapable. It was the $trillions of opaque securities, not the $billions guaranteed by the government that brought the world's financial system to its knees. The mentality of "get rich quick" that had begun with Milken has expanded dramatically. With the creation of the asset-backed securities market, speculative finance has threatened the livelihood of average people even beyond what Milken and his raiders had imposed on them. The entire economic system is now so imbedded with the new way of thinking that it may very well be that unacceptable unemployment levels are not going away, despite the fact that the economy has been recovering for quite some time now. For one thing, banks would rather create another bubble in the market, as they've been doing since 2008, rather than loan the money that the Fed has been putting on their books to small businesses and individuals. For another, corporate CEO's, who are now truly a part of the new system, play ball by focusing on quarterly returns rather than focusing on long term plans which would require an expansion of their labor force. Headlines such as "No Rush To Hire Even As Profits Soar," which appeared in the Wall Street Journal in February, 2011, are becoming increasingly common.

Defining The New Model

Making one's fortune now takes precedence over acting responsibly. It's not even a question that's considered. This is what the new financial model is all about.

In the older Wall Street model, investment bankers provided advice to corporate CEO's and individual investors, and in return were compensated by the fees that they charged.[90] Milken and Ranieri changed all this. From the 1980's on, traders have come to see the fabulous possibilities presented by takeovers and by securitization. In Charles Gasparino's words,

> Young MBA's no longer wanted to advise CEO's how to run their businesses; they wanted to use leverage to take over the companies, restructure their operations and sell them at a profit.[91]

---

90   Gasparino, *The Sellout*, p.25.

91   Ibid., p.16.

Brokerage firms no longer had an interest in recommending safe, long term investments;

> They made their fortunes by churning the accounts of their customers, essentially trading shares they didn't need in order to generate commissions. Bankers didn't buy their second home in the Hamptons simply simply by telling a company how to manage its cash flow; the trick was to get the typical CEO in the 1980's to grow a company by acquisitions, often using debt to finance the deal.[92]

The secret is now out for those with ambition. Either use bonds to buy a corporation, or securitize consumer loans. Or, if you're of a mind to, speculate in oil. These three paths, each in their own way, have wreaked havoc with the middle class, which has become the chief victim of Wall Street's new game.

It's interesting to note that the percentage of new jobs created in the first decade of the 21st century, as reported by the Bureau of Labor Statistics, is zero percent, despite the rampaging markets and the feeling of prosperity they engendered for almost seven years. Zero percent! All the job gains made in the market bubble were lost when the bubble burst. How could wages ever grow with zero percent job growth? They

---

92   Ibid..

can't. Job growth was supposed to be the major justification for all of this new financial activity. Even Smick, despite his wary eye, states,

> Over the last quarter century, America has championed the bipartisan concept that open markets, a turbocharged entrepreneurial capitalism, and freely flowing international capital markets represent a magical formula for economic success.[93]

Unfortunately they don't. Belief in magical formulas and turbocharged growth is the reason why, to our great regret, the smart money bet on the hare instead of the tortoise. The more one reflects on what has happened the thinner and thinner the defense for this new system becomes.

---

93 Smick, *The World Is Curved*, p. 29.

Chapter 4.
Why It's Not China

The only financial advance that
has benefited consumers is the
ATM machine.
Paul Volker, former Fed Chairman

Eliminating Other Possibilities

Recently, we asked our students what they thought about the impact of China on the US economy. The question was posed this way: "How many of you believe that Chinese imports are responsible for the declining living standard of the American middle class?" There was a little hesitancy at first, then slowly hands began to rise. Soon, every hand was up; courage had overtaken shyness and the vote became unanimous.

The students' response was what we had expected, so after expressing their opinion, we then asked them to look at the list of fifteen countries that had been placed on the board. Next to each country was a coefficient number that measured how income is distributed in varying nations.

Once the meaning of the coefficients was explained, it became immediately obvious that among the high income countries on the list, only two nations were trending significantly towards rising income inequality. These were the United States and the United Kingdom, not coincidently, the only two countries that had significantly deregulated their financial markets in the 1970's, 80's and 90's. Very significantly, it was also obvious that the trend toward this inequality had been set in motion in the late 1970's, twenty-five years before China had any real impact on the American economy.

It's important to note that the measurements, which we will discuss, did not cover any of the twenty-first century, the period when China's impact truly became noticeable. The students quickly picked up on this fact, smiling in recognition of the point we were making. China's impact on the way our incomes are currently distributed only looks important if you restrict your measurements to this century. And like China, the decline began too early to be blamed on new technologies since they came on line after the decline was already underway.

DOES THIS ALL mean that China has not raised problems for American workers? No, not at all. They've added to the problem. It's becoming increasingly clear that the speed of Chinese development makes it very difficult for American workers to adjust to the Asian outsourcing we have been experiencing.[94] Industries

---

94   *"Tallying The Toll of US-China Trade".*, Wall Street Journal, Sept. 27, 2011.

such as textiles, apparel, electronic equipment and computers have all enjoyed spectacular growth in China at the expense of American workers. A recent study done in Raleigh and in Cleveland make the negative effects of Chinese imports very clear. Areas in these cities with the greatest exposure to Chinese imports have working populations that were more adversely affected than those in other work areas in the same cities.[95]

The speed of Chinese development has overwhelmed the ability of workers to resettle into equivalent jobs. But even considering this, if we restore our trade balance with China, it will not reverse our trend toward rising income inequality. Nor will it reverse the decline in middle class incomes that has been occurring, because the continuous decline of the middle class is directly proportional to the rise in incomes that is occurring at the top. The two are different sides of the same coin. Growing inequality is the trend that has accompanied the mergers and acquisitions movement.

The altering of American corporate culture that occurred with Milken, which became so clear in the 1980's is the only explanation consistent with the changes that have occurred in middle class incomes. Milken and his raiders made corporations lean and mean. Not lean and mean for shareholders, but rather lean and mean for the work force. This is the core

---

95   Ibid.

reason why the American middle class has been under continuous pressure. The environment they work in is hostile to their interests. It's hostile to everyone in fact, except to shareholders. The facts become clear when we look at what the numbers say.

Gini Coefficients And The Story They Tell

Gini coefficients are concept functions commonly used to measure income distribution trends, measuring inequality on a scale of 0 to 1. When at 0, the coefficient represents perfect equality, and when at 1, perfect inequality. When applying an interpretation to these coefficients, a country with a Gini coefficient of 0.28 is considered to have a very equitable distribution of incomes while a nation with a 0.50 would be considered a disaster in this category. In the 0.40 range, societies are in a zone where inequities begin to become very obvious and consequently unsettling politically. It is through these coefficient numbers that we can see the erosion of the US's income distribution since the mid 1970's. The graph below depicts this. Notice how the coefficients rise as the "takeover movement" gains momentum in the 1980's. Notice also how clear the trend became in the 80's and how it continued to rise in the 90's and then on into the present century, until it reached the now unenviable level of approximately 0.45. As of 2011, it continues to rise.

See the chart below.

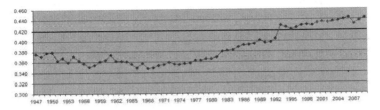

Gini Index in U.S. 1947-2009[96]
Source: Census Bureau

When Milken's work began, the US Gini Coefficient was slightly under 0.36, a number that was very similar to what the equality conscious Western Europeans were experiencing.[97] By 1993, the new corporate culture had become embedded in the economy and the US Gini coefficient rose to 0.43, compared to 0.30 for Germany. France, Italy, Canada and Japan all showed similar low numbers.[98] Our present coefficient of .45 puts us more in line with Latin America than with our European counterparts. Countries such as Bolivia, Uruguay and Ecuador are in this range, a fact which is disturbing because we don't consider ourselves to be in a league that is comparable to the middle-income nations of Latin American. At 0.45, we are rapidly approaching the income disparities of nations such as Peru, which at 0.49 has been in a constant state of

96   http://www.census.gov/hhes/www/income/data/historical/inequality/f04.xls

97   See the graph pictured at the indicated website. http://en.wikipedia.org/wiki/Gini_coefficient

98   Ibid.

revolution for decades. These countries are all oligarchies, ruled by political and economic elites, hardly the type of nations towards which we should be trending.[99]

Along these same lines, *The Wall Street Journal* recently reported that although Americans still move up and down the economic ladder,

> there is evidence they are doing so
> less often than they used to, and
> less often than residents of Canada
> and Western Europe.[100]

Except for the UK, hostile takeovers are difficult to engineer in all of Western Europe and Japan. Germany, Europe's key player, uses laws called poison pills to prevent takeovers. In Japan, hostile takeovers are not possible because of the cross ownership that exists between government, banks, and the multiple corporations that make up the Japanese Kieretsu system.

The chart below shows just how rapidly inequality has been rising in the US.[101] Note that in the 1970's, we were on a par with Europe and Japan. Note also how this situation had changed rather dramatically by the

---

99   Baumol, William, Robert Litan and Carl Schramm. *Good Capitalism/Bad Capitalism: And The economics of Growth With Prosperity*. New Haven: Yale University Press, 2005, p.72

100   "Income Ladder's Sticky Steps", *The Wall Street Journal,* Saturday/Sunday, November 12-13, 2011, p. A4..

101   See Baumol, et. al., *Good Capitalism/Bad Capitalism,* pp. 72-73.

time we reached 1990. By 2000, we came to resemble oligarchic capitalist systems, such as those existing in Latin America. This is something our economists have yet to call attention to.

COUNTRY	1970 Gini #	1980 Gini #	1990 Gini #	2000 Gini #	2010 Gini #
Japan	.35	.32	.25 (1993)		
Germany	.33	.32	.32	.28	
France	.45	.35	.32 (1995)	.34	
Italy	.42	.35	.34		
UK	.24	.25	.31	.36(1999)	
US	**.35**	**.38**	**.40**	**43**	**.45**
Bolivia			.45		
Peru				.49	
Uruguay				.45	
Venezuela				.49	

These figures reflect what is becoming recognizable in everyday American life. The Wall Street protestors who were of a serious mind may be a motley group representing a myriad of confused ideologies, but they know enough to point the finger at the people who are most responsible for these trends.

Resisting The Obvious

Since the trend in US income distribution runs head on with the image we have of ourselves as the world's most successful middle class nation, the question arises as to why economists haven't set themselves to analyzing these issues? And why haven't free-market commentators been willing to look at the imposing growth of Wall Street as a potential source of our growing inequality? In the course of our research, only Kevin Phillips called attention to the fact that economists have studiously avoided the impact of hostile takeovers on the incomes of average people.[102] Free market economists continue to cling to the notion that only governments cause economic problems. Why is this?

We believe this resistance is related to the fact that the beauty of an idea, such as the belief that markets always clear away problems if left alone, is so pleasing to the mind that we resist all the challenges that reality throws at these assumptions. Whether economists be capitalists or socialists, they will cling to the purity of their ideas and resist accepting what's obviously true no matter what prevailing circumstances point to. Economists will manipulate data until it fits comfortably into their model because their ideology represents an idea that removes all of the complexity and contradictions that are a part of our real life experience. The result is an ideology that becomes a mantra, repeated over and over until it creates a harmony of thought that unfortunately over simplifies complex issues. So we are told that the singular cause of the collapse of a global financial system worth hundreds of $trillions was the $200 billion worth of sub-prime mortgages that Fannie Mae and Freddie Mac forced onto the banking system.

102　See Phillips, *Bad Money*.

The stubbornness that many market economists have shown in defending Wall Street has a lot to do with turning economic models into dogma. We don't need to deny the logic of the market system in order to support the need for market regulation. It's the quest for ideological purity that stands in the way.

In any case, our suggestion of an over-zealous commitment to ideology is one way to account for the strange avoidance of the facts that Gini Coefficients make so obvious. That Wall Street now earns almost half of the nation's profits, while producing none of the goods or services counted by the GDP, should itself be enough to sound alarm bells. The fact that the Congressional Budget Office reports that the top 1% have tripled their wealth over the last thirty years should also sound alarms.[103] And so should the fact that Wall Street, in order to insure its interests, now employs five lobbyists for every member of Congress. Clearly, we have entered a new economic era, one where the nation's economy is dominated by finance, the sector that once served as the mere handmaiden to the economy. This is not healthy for a nation that prides itself on its democracy.

103   *Providence Journal*, October 29, 2011, p. C4.

Chapter 5.
Oil- The Story Of How Fuel Fell Under Wall Street's Control

In May 2004. . .we constructed an
elaborate oil price regression model
that showed the equilibrium or fair
value price of oil at $32.48 to be
ridiculously precise. Most energy
experts maintained it was even lower,
pricing out in the high $20s.
Hedge Hogging, Barton Biggs

When Price Became Divorced From The Fundamentals Of Supply and Demand

Something very strange happened in 2008. As a result of the sub-prime mortgage collapse, people lost their jobs, consumer demand fell, stock prices tumbled, and the drop in economic activity caused world petroleum supplies to rise to historically high levels. Yet, with one calamity piling up on top of another, the price of oil raced from the vicinity of $30/barrel to $147. Why? Why would the price of oil rise to historic levels, eventually pushing gasoline to $4/gallon, when there was no threat to oil supplies and when world demand was contracting?

It's been suggested by market purists that the depreciation of the dollar led to the price spike, but surely a 12% dollar depreciation would not translate into a 400% price rise. This makes no sense. What is interesting to note, however, is the fact that free market economists had the good sense to stay away from explanations based on the price fundamentals of supply and demand because they know that world conditions should have pushed a barrel of oil even lower than the $32.48/barrel price that Barton Biggs' hedge fund had placed it at in 2004 (see opening quote). At a $147/barrel, something had gone very wrong with the oil pricing mechanism.

IN 2008, THE year oil prices took off, the world's inventory of oil was constantly at or near full capacity. Strategic reserves were full too. There was plainly no problem with supply. Nor was the demand situation pressuring prices. The US, along with Western Europe had descended into a deep recession, and the Japanese economy had been flat since the middle of the 1990's. Even Chinese growth was slowing. So why was oil spiking?

The quick and most plausible answer is that demand for oil was being distorted by speculators in New York, where huge bets were being placed on the NYMEX (New York Mercantile Exchange), and on other exchanges where virtually all US oil is bought and sold today. Oil speculators, those financiers who buy and sell oil contracts without any intention of ever taking possession of the product, were, and remain at the heart of the price problem because they have harnessed huge concentrations of wealth and poured it into the oil markets, completely distorting the nation's average demand for oil.

For example, in 2003, when Wall Street was focused on the mortgage and securities markets, investment banks, hedge funds, and pension funds had purchased only $13 billion worth of oil. By 2008, that figure had risen twenty times, to $260 billion worth of purchases.[104] This is what completely threw market demand off kilter. It turned out that in 2008, when oil prices rose to historic levels, a full 81% of all oil contracts sold had been purchased by the big funds on speculation.[105] It's the reason why oil, which should have been selling at $30.00 or so per barrel in July of 2008 was actually selling at $147 a barrel. It also explains why in December of the same year oil plunged, settling at $33/barrel.[106] There's money to be made in shorting oil just as there is in buying it long.

NOT VERY LONG ago, most oil transactions were handled by small distributors who connected the oil in tankers and in pipelines with the companies that use the product. Twenty years ago, the oil market was still highly decentralized, and prices reasonably

104   David Cho, "A Few Speculators Dominate Vast Market For Oil Trading". *Washington Post*, August 21, 2008.

105   Ibid.

106   Taibbi, *Griftopia*, p. 150.

reflected global supply and demand. That's all changed. Today, the US oil market is centered in New York and London, where the big financial houses, with government assistance, have been able to gain complete control of the trade. The story is actually very similar to what happened in the housing market, where the small, decentralized lending institutions came to be plugged into Wall Street banks, which quickly distorted prices with their enormous purchases of mortgages, precipitated the housing bubble, which they then pricked by betting against the very mortgage bonds they had rolled all those mortgages into. Like housing, ultimate control of oil prices has passed from small institutions to big investment firms that can pile on demand and precipitate price bubbles whenever it suits their interest.

BEFORE WE MOVE on to the specifics of this argument, it may be useful to describe two interviews that took place on the Bloomberg radio broadcasts of "The Hayes Advantage." On April 30, 2011, the moderator, Kathleen Hayes, was speaking with John Olson, a money manager. During the course of the interview, Olson explained that oil prices now follow the Standard & Poors index, not consumer demand. What Olson meant was the oil market is no longer a separate, decentralized entity. It is integrated into all of Wall Street's operations. Confirming this, Olson went on to note that when demand for oil is down, and the stock market is up, oil prices will rise (because they follow the market rather than the normal channels of supply and demand).

To what level will they rise? On the same show a month earlier, on March 28, Steven Short of the hedge fund, Short Group, answered this question. Short noted that he had shorted oil in the middle of the Libyan uprising because if it rose significantly higher than the $101/barrel price it was selling at, it would threaten the American economy, losing investment firms money in other areas. So he expected the price rise would not exceed $115/barrel. The implication here, of course, is that the financial sector uses its power to set the various markets it participates in at levels that can maximize its revenues. Financial operations like these now make the idea that oil prices operate independently of the financial sector seem almost quaint.

For those who remain in doubt, consider the obvious question. If oil's price is not being controlled by the big investment funds, how could an insider like Short know that the price was being pegged to its impact level on the American economy? Even more to the point, if the Egyptian-Libyan-Syrian uprisings were really the cause of oil's rise in 2011, why would Mr. Short be betting that the price was going to fall right in the middle of a crisis? As the interview continued, Short noted that at $115/barrel, consumers would be spending five cents of every dollar they have on gasoline, while at $100/barrel they would be spending only four cents/dollar.

It was this difference that was making speculators worry about oil's potential impact on other markets. There was nothing in Short's discussion to indicate that oil's price was based on the potential threat to supply created by the Mid-East uprisings, even though this was the press' and the public's general assumption. Both Short and Olson spoke as if everyone in Hayes' audience understood that the big investors were the ones that moved oil prices. Amazing! Even more amazing is the fact that no attention is called to this fact, even though gasoline now sells at $3.50/gallon rather than at the $1.50/gallon it sold at in the first half of the new century.

It's The New System

It's worth remembering at this point that we're not suggesting that some monopolistic cabal exists on Wall Street where fund managers sit in dark lounges conspiring to raise and lower prices. Remember, Mr. Short was betting against those speculators who thought prices would still be rising when he shorted oil(betting it would fall). The funds move on their own research and intelligence, although they certainly will follow the movement of others, and the giants will sometimes make plays to get the smaller funds to follow.

What we're really talking about is a new system, one that now allows big banks and funds to bend the oil markets because of the vast sums they are now allowed to invest in these markets. Previously, heavy speculating in commodities and oil was illegal. It no longer is.[107] In this new system, big individual investors have a newly found financial power that enables them to stampede oil markets. The big players take advantage of opportunities independently of each other, but their purchases and sales have the power to induce others to pile on. Collaboration is not necessary. When the big players decide to pile on, the others follow.

WHAT IS IT that makes the thesis of price manipulation by speculators seem plausible? Mostly the numbers. They show the dramatic increase in oil speculation. We've mentioned that the purchase of oil contracts rose from $13 billion in 2003 to $260 billion in 2008. For this to have happened, a number of changes had to occur. For one, the once decentralized oil markets had to be centralized, preferably in New York, and placed into the hands of huge funds that move high impact sums of money. A strategy for moving these sums of money was also needed, while at the same time, the nation's formidable restrictions on trading commodities had to be overturned. But even before any of this could happen, Wall Street had to be convinced that serious money could be made through this type of speculative trading. The first obstacle to be overcome was to end Wall Street's suspicion of speculation.

---

107   Just how this market was deregulated will be part of our discussion later in this chapter..

The End of "Efficient Markets Theory"

Lest we forget, there once was a time when financiers were a staid, conservative group who invested their clients money in a very prudent way. By temperament, investors were a conservative bunch, willing to tie their investment decisions to a theory that was referred to as "Efficient Markets Theory."[108]

In its briefest form, efficient markets theory held that all goods were priced as they should be, according to the dictates of cost, just as the micro-economics text-books said they were. And if the markets priced goods efficiently, they also priced securities efficiently. So what was there to speculate on? Better to aim for a 9%/yearly return, and make a decent living, than hopelessly gamble on price swings, and lose. The market reflected the true value of the nation's companies, and these values were not prone to wild movements.

Up until the late 1980's, efficient markets theory held sway throughout the investment world. The hypothesis was taught in all of our colleges and universities, and spawned a generation of professors and students who brought these ideas to New York. Markets perfectly reflected the value of goods. Demand was exactly aligned with supply, which in turn was an accurate reflection of costs. It was believed that only these factors determined a company's worth, and further, that this worth was accurately reflected in stock prices. So what was to be gained by

---

108   Sebastian Mallaby, *More Money Than God,* New York: The Penguin Group, 2010, pp.5-7.

speculating, especially in the US, where information flowed flawlessly through markets? Whenever information on products changed even slightly, smart investors pounced on that information, readjusting prices to where they should be. Efficient markets theory had no loopholes. It was tight as a drum.[109]

IN THE 1970'S, it was still widely believed that hedge fund managers were cowboys, operating on the erroneous assumption that they could beat the efficiency of market pricing.[110] Why should a bank loan a hedge fund 50,000 shares of Ford on the hunch that it was overpriced and should be shorted when you yourself didn't believe it was overpriced? Nor did lending hedge funds $100 million to buy Ford long make any sense either. Markets were too efficient to engage in this type of leveraging. You might as well take a "Random Walk Down Wall Street," or have a monkey throw dots at a stock sheet as try to find areas where the markets had overvalued or undervalued securities. All relevant information had already been taken into account and was embedded in the price of the securities that were traded.

Then came the shocking crash of October 19, 1987. It caused stunned investors to immediately jettison their commitment to the theory, and once they did this, they never looked back. If the bottom could fall out the way it did in a single day, then market

---

109   Ibid.

110   Ibid., p. 7.

prices were relative. With losses like those incurred when the market fell, it suddenly became difficult to argue that market prices were objectively set by fundamentals. They now appeared to be based as much on whim and momentum as on anything else. As it turned out, this reasoning was music to the ears of those with a gambler's instinct.

The sudden change in thinking was quickly adopted by university professors. Larry Summers, who would eventually advise both Presidents Clinton and Obama, jested with a fellow Harvard colleague at the time that

> The stock in the efficient markets
> hypothesis . . . crashed [on that day]
> along with the rest of the market.[111]

Throughout the country, financial scholars now turned their attention to the new ideas that would soon be resonating throughout the financial world.[112] Those with a true gambler's instinct began to see the markets as something to be played like a roulette wheel, except that if you were very intelligent, you could turn the odds in your favor. One of the nation's chief economists, Paul Samuelson suddenly recognized the potential power of hedge funds, whose use of borrowed securities could make untold fortunes by

---

111   Mallaby, *More Money Than God,* p. 7

112   Justin Fox details this entire transformation in his work *The Myth of the Rational Market,* New York, Harper Collins, 2009

using this leverage as they combined buying long and hedging short on the advice of the nation's most brilliant students.

After the crash, Samuelson formed his own hedge fund, Commodities Corporation or CC, along with Helmut Weymar, a former star cocoa trader.[113] CC's approach to investing in commodities represented the new revolutionary approach that was now being launched.

> The management at CC had a solid understanding of risk taking and offered an incredibly open framework in which traders thrived.[114]
> [italics mine]

CC went on to serve as an important source of funding for many of the future hedge funds that would be trading in commodities like oil.[115]

Another example of the expression of new attitudes was seen with the formation of the soon to be famous (or infamous) hedge fund, LTCM (Long Term Capital Management). This firm, heavily involved in the crash of the Asian currency markets in the late 1990's, was created in 1994 with a staff recruited as much for their intelligence as for their trading skills. They were "an all star cast of financial minds"[116] who,

---

113   Drobny, *Inside the House of Money,* p.9.

114   Ibid., p.9.

115   Ibid.

116   Ibid., p.24.

like Samuelson, believed they could develop quantitative formulas that could beat the markets big time.

The problem with the rising popularity of hedge funds was that they had the ability to leverage huge sums that could drive markets into dramatic swings. Today, the rough-neck mentality of hedge funds is not looked upon as a negative. Instead, it has made them the new super stars of the wild-cat operations that currently define our markets.

AFTER 1987, INSTITUTIONAL money from pension funds, insurance funds, mutual funds and investment banks began to pour into hedge funds because their returns were averaging a startling 20%, a return that led to a doubling of that investment every three and one half years. In 1990, the total assets rose to $30 billion, a large number, but it was still only the beginning. Fifteen years later, assets under hedge fund management reached $1.2 trillion, and by 2008, the figure stood at a cool $2 trillion.[117] This is the kind of capital that has an enormous effect on the power to escalate demand in the oil markets, and to de-escalate it as well. Just the Over the Counter or OTC trade in "swaps", a type of derivative which includes bets on oil, grew from being too rare to be measured in 1990 to over $3 trillion in market value by 2008. If measured at their

---

117   Simon Johnson and James Kwak, *13 Bankers: The Wall Street Takeover and the Next Financial Meltdown*. New York: Pantheon Books, 2010, p. 78.

face value, the value of the swaps market reached an astounding $680 trillion before the collapse.[118]

When derivatives are used in the oil markets, they are referred to as "rate swaps." What's interesting about rate swaps is the fact that they do not represent the actual purchase of oil. They are simply side bets, placed on the contracts that have been placed to buy oil that will be delivered at a future date. The problem is oil prices follow the prices of the contracts that these side bets influence.[119] It's as if a group of ten thousand strangers, who have no share in your home's ownership, were able to buy fire insurance policies on the policy you yourself have on your house. As the demand for these insurance policies push their price up, the sale value of your policy rises, and by inference, the value of your house. So too with the rate swaps that place bets on oil contracts.

Very little is known about this swaps market because it operates in what is referred to as the shadow banking system, beyond the reach of government regulations. But we do know how it works. Rate swaps are really secondary derivatives which place bets on the primary futures contracts, betting on where their price will move to as they are bought and sold by speculators. The information these speculators use to place their purchases is mostly from the prices the rate swaps are being traded at. Since these swaps are themselves speculated on, it's

---

118   Ibid., p.10.
119   Cho, "A Few Speculators"

a complex market entered into only by those with experience and a cool head. This whole, unregulated system, which we referred to as a shadow banking system, is larger than the regulated banking system. It trades derivatives such as RMBS', CDO's, and swaps in the $hundreds of trillions and nothing is monitored.

In the case of rate swaps, the point of buying and selling them is commissions, commissions that grow as the price rises. They allow huge sums to be invested in oil, sums much larger than the value of the oil itself that's being sold. With oil prices following the price of these derivatives, rate swaps are able to take demand wherever the momentum of fund purchases take it. Best of all, traders never have the worry of taking possession of the product, since these derivatives are secondary securities. How far we've come from the prudent trading environment that characterized Wall Street in its sober days, when "efficient markets theory" held sway. Markets today are often intricate, arcane, and understood in depth by only a few. And they deal in sums that allow the financial sector to impact demand in ways that the traders of the 1980's could only have dreamed of.

Running Money From Market To Market

The new investing mentality that emerged in 1987 fit perfectly into the numerous markets that had been emerging since the early 1970's. One of these markets, the currency market, was created by President Nixon when he unpegged the dollar from gold. The great merit of the new currency system was that it was intended to keep trade between nations in balance. If, for example, we began to import more goods from Japan, far in excess of what they were willing to buy from us, the extra demand placed on their currency would raise its value, making their goods more expensive- which would then make them less desirable. What quickly happened, however, was currency traders began to speculate on the direction a currency's value might take. By the 1990's, speculation had reached a point where huge currency selloffs destroyed entire economies.

Trading in these years also expanded into asset-backed securities, and into the secondary derivatives written on these securities. It was the beginning of the party that caused a global recession and which continues to this day, even with more added features. We now see secondary derivatives written on all commodities, ranging from food to fibers and to oil, all of these being a vital part of the middle-class budget. Where once the movement of big money was limited to a back-and- forth sway between stocks and bonds, it now trades in a number of new markets whose creation resembles the building of new casinos. They bring nothing positive to the community they supposedly serve, but they are very lucrative for those who own and run the game.

ONE OF THE first by-products of these new investment possibilities was the appearance of a strategy that centered on the creation of "boom and bust" cycles both on a national and international level. Hedge fund managers quickly used the 90's as a training ground for the movement of money from market to market. By the time the century ended, traders had figured out a system where they could make formerly undreamed of profits by creating a bubble in one market, crashing it, and with their expanding funds repeat the process in other markets. No area escaped the sharp eyes of hedge funds and investment banks like Goldman-Sachs. By the 2000's, oil came to fit perfectly into this new strategy.

The US, and in fact the entire global economy, was pushed into a perpetual bubble/collapse mode as soon as the hedge funds gained enough clout to influence demand. By 1993, for example, George Soros' hedge fund was able to successfully attack the British pound when it forced the British Treasury to devalue its currency. Incredible as it seems, a single individual holding no office now had enough financial clout to push an advanced nation around with nothing but profit as a motive. It was a portent of things to come. A year later, a currency crisis occurred in Mexico that required a $50 billion US bailout. Then Speaker of the House, Newt Gingrich, called the Mexican crisis the first real-time global emergency brought on by the new global economy.[120] He could have added that it was the first

---

120   Daniel Yergen, *Commanding Heights, a DVD based on a book by the same title.*

real time example of how Wall Street would be crashing markets everywhere, because there was a laundry list of crashes that followed. A bond market rout in the US, like the attack on the British pound, also came in 1993. Later in the decade, the world watched spellbound as the banks and hedge funds crashed all of the Asian "tiger" economies. The Asian currency crises of 1997 struck Thailand first, destroying the nation's entire economy. It then moved on to Malaysia, where it did the same. Indonesia's currency fell next, bringing riots and social turmoil to that country. Then the seemingly impossible happened. The panic spread to a high income nation, South Korea, putting it in desperate need of an emergency cash infusion to avoid collapse. Russia, which came next, was unable to stave off the speculators and the ruble collapsed. The IMF attempted to intervene by injecting huge sums of dollars into Russia, but the remedy failed. Only a few really know where all our taxpayer money ended up. Eventually, the dumping of currencies which began in Thailand reached the shores of Connecticut, where it threatened to bankrupt the international hedge fund, Long Term Capital Management (LTCM). So vast was LTCM's involvement in the currency derivatives market that it had to be saved by New York bankers who feared that its collapse would trigger a global recession. As it turned out, their actions only postponed what was rapidly becoming inevitable.

After the collapse of national currencies, the dotcom companies that grew rapidly in the 1990's saw their stocks taken to wild speculative heights. PE's or price to earnings ratios for some tech stocks rose as high as 5,000, which was 200 times higher than what was historically thought to be a safe level. But the public was assured by some who were supposedly in the know that high PE's for dot com stocks weren't the same as they were for other stocks. Just why the same rules didn't apply was never explained. When the bubble that this run up created finally burst, the process was repeated for the entire market, which crashed at the turn of the century. This crash had been helped along by companies like Enron, World Dot Com., and Arthur Anderson, all of which gave the American public their first real look at just how corrupt much of Wall Street had become. As we all know, the mortgage market came next.

AS THE NEW century dawned, Alan Greenspan's Federal Reserve, and then Ben Bernanke's Fed pumped increasing amounts of money into the banks, leading them to understand that there would be no price to pay for dangerous speculation. The money that the Fed released quickly moved into property. As we have seen, Wall Street's sale of mortgage bonds created the environment that led to the property bubble that emerged around 2005.

Writer Steven Drobny has noted that Alan Greenspan seemed to interpret his role as

> needing to intervene only as the
> party goers are stumbling home.
> As he has claimed, bubbles can

only be clearly observed in hind-
sight.[121]

Surely the Chairman was jesting. It was he, himself, who had said the markets were suffering from
"irrational exuberance" during the late 90's bubble.
The problem was Greenspan's libertarian sympathies
were with the banks. He was, if not actually in league
with them, certainly one of their biggest fans. As one
critic has noted,

> The financial services industry inflated
> one speculative bubble after another, and
> each time the bubble burst, Greenspan and
> the Fed swept in to save the day by printing
> vast sums of money and dumping it back on
> Wall Street, in effect encouraging people
> to drink themselves sober.[122]

By keeping key interest rates at or near zero, the
Fed kept and continues to keep the big banks flushed
with the money they need to fund these bubbles. This
is how Wall Street was able to move enormous sums
of money, even after the global crash, into the commodities markets, and most especially into oil.

In fairness to the Fed, easy money is exactly what
the times called for in 2008. It was following a long
approved recipe when it pumped money into the banks
in exchange for as many of the toxic assets that money

---

121   Drobny, *Inside The House of Money,* p. 13.

122   Ibid., p. 53

could buy. The Fed rightly expected the money would be loaned to companies for expansion. The problem was (and remains) the big banks have developed an appetite for easy money made the new modern way. So they directed a large portion of this money into the oil markets that had been created on the NYMEX, and into derivatives called "rate swaps", which are bets on the oil contracts bought on the NYMEX. Had the money gone, as it was intended, to corporations so it could speed up an end to this stubborn employment market, our nagging unemployment would have dried up. Today, it's taken for granted that the money being pumped into the economy essentially benefits the wealthy. Even conservative economist Holman Jenkins of The Wall Street Journal noted in a 2013 column that

> The rich derive their incomes disproportionately from assets, and the Fed's explicit contribution has been to boost asset prices.[123]

To this day, many economists continue to wait for the inflation all this money will create, overlooking the fact it has created inflation, in the market. That's why the market is again at an all-time high. They have also overlooked the fact that the commodities markets, and most especially oil, have been inflated for the last five years, just as stocks have.

---

123   Holman W. Jenkins Jr., "Rewriting the Lehman Postmortem", *Wall Street Journal,* Saturday/Sunday, September 21-22, 2013.

BUT HOW DOES one get away with creating bubbles in the oil market, where one would think public scrutiny is at its sharpest?

The answer is as financiers grew wealthier and bolder, they came to discover a great truth, one they had never suspected, although politicians were long familiar with the phenomenon. To their unbelieving eyes, fund managers and bankers came to realize that the American public had a very high tolerance for being pushed around, and for being snookered. The public rarely analyses what the press is saying.[124] You have a barrel of oil rising in price by 400% in the middle of a recession? Tell the public it's because the dollar has devalued 12%. They'll accept the argument with a nod. Just run a few strategic headlines like *"Dollars Continued Slide Forces Oil Up Again,"* and the explanation will go unchallenged. Finance found it was like taking candy from a baby as they added oil to the series of markets that are now regularly turned into bubbles. But before they were able to trade in high volume, however, they had to create a commodities market where oil could be bought and sold by big speculators. This proved to be surprisingly more difficult than New York had originally thought.

---

124   Later in this chapter, we will see Mike Taibbi's statements on this point as he and his fellow reporters covered candidates McCain and Obama..

How Oil Became A New Market For The Big Players

When the belief in efficient markets theory ended, investment banks such as Goldman-Sachs began to position themselves for entry into the oil markets. Before that could be done, however, certain obstacles had to be overcome. First, major investors faced the reality that there was no central market place where oil could be bought and sold. Second, the banks and funds faced the problem of stiff government regulations on speculation in commodities such as oil. Finally, speculators were about to deal with a product whose supply had become very predictable after the 1970's. Predictability isn't good for speculators because they need to make bets on commodities whose supply is unpredictable.[125] All of this meant that oil, unlike food, was not a good fit for a futures market. Nevertheless, a handful of speculators decided to give it a try and in the early 70's they turned to the NYMEX, a small commodities exchange that had been operating rather unsuccessfully in lower Manhattan.

---

125   Commodities fall into a special category of products that are very vulnerable to price swings because supplies are not easily controlled. Foods are sold as "commodities" because farmers learned long ago that selling a crop not yet harvested at a guaranteed price was safer than running the risk that prices would rise above the average, because too often bumper crops pushed them below the average. Since speculators were quite willing to buy a future crop at its average price in the hope it would rise, farmers passed off the gamble to them.

THE NYMEX, OR New York Mercantile Exchange, was, in the 1970's, a relatively small commodities exchange, selling mostly butter and eggs in arbitrage trading with the Chicago Commodities Exchange.[126] In the 70's, traders on the NYMEX had hoped to help their fledging market along by adding products such as Maine potatoes to their list. But the trade never quite got off the ground, so in 1978, when a young twenty seven year old named Michael Marks joined NYMEX's board of directors, attention was turned to establishing a ring[127] for the buying and selling of oil.[128]

It was a very hard sell. Big oil companies showed no interest in dealing with oil futures. It made no sense to them to buy oil that hadn't yet been pumped out of the ground. They had their distributors. Why should they need oil traders? Consequently, traders on the NYMEX were reduced to using the yellow pages to find home heating oil companies who were willing to buy and sell on a futures arrangement with their customers, hoping they would be willing to "lock in" for the winter season.[129]

---

126   Emily Lambert, *The Futures, the Rise of the Speculator and the Origins of the World's Biggest Markets,* New York: Basic Books, The Perseus Books Group, 2011, pp. 155-157

127   In Chicago, each commodity is sold in a lowered platform called a "pit", while in New York, each commodity is sold in what is called a "ring", an open space with a large table for traders to lean on. See Lambert, *The Futures, pp 155-157*

128   Ibid., PP 127-128.

129   Ibid.

Obviously, finding customers from the yellow pages was not a very lucrative affair, and for a long while this activity did nothing more than provide a foothold for would be oil traders. The big break that made real speculation in oil possible on the NYMEX occurred when the Federal government gave investment banks permission to take huge speculative positions in commodities. We'll describe how this came about, but for now let's simply say that once the government deregulated the market speculation on the NYMEX took off, and traders never looked back.

Ben Mezrich, writing about his own experiences at the NYMEX in 2007, describes just how profitable oil became.

> Vitzi grinned. The excess of the evening [at a nightclub called Green Tea] was a point of pride to him, especially because he knew that word of the night's spending spree would move across the trading floor faster than he'd been spreading drinks around the VIP room. Vitzi certainly didn't care about the money: He had made $500,000 profit that morning. Half a million wasn't a record for the Merc Exchange, but it was a pretty damn impressive take.[130]

---

130   Ben Mezrich, *Rigged*, New York, Harper Collins, 2007, p. 5.

The pioneers who sold heating oil to the "mom and pop" companies and saved the NYMEX in the process could, after 2008, be thanked for making the high life possible for traders like "Vitzi." By successfully putting oil on the exchange, the early oil traders gave the big players who came later the centralized exchange they needed to place the bets that now cost consumers so much money.

Government Deregulation: That Last Piece Of The Puzzle

BY 2000, ALL of the pieces for gaining control of the oil markets were slowly coming into place. Investors had developed the will to speculate, a market-to-market bubble strategy that oil fit into perfectly had developed, and now the NYMEX was there to handle centralized purchasing. There was only one obstacle left, and that was government regulation.

Since the New Deal, both federal and state government had tied the hands of speculators in the commodities markets. They faced hurdles everywhere, with the biggest going all the way back to the 1930's, when it was decided by Congress that commodities speculators had been involved in numerous abuses, "speculative orgies" as they termed them. Congress believed that speculators had driven agricultural prices down to bankruptcy levels, pointing to speculators like Arthur Cutten, a Chicago trader who was responsible for several massive attacks on the commodity markets before moving to New York.[131] He came to symbolize everything that average people in the 1930's came to hate. Whether people like Cutter deserved to be vilified is an open question, but Congress was of one mind on the subject. He helped move them to pass the Commodity Exchange Act of 1936, which severely curtailed speculation in commodities. Until it was removed, it made profitable speculating in oil impossible because it limited speculative positions to approximately 20% of all commodities transactions.

Then, 1987 came, destroying "efficient markets theory" and justifying speculative gambling. If speculators were going to make real money, even with the NYMEX in place, it was necessary to get those position limits removed. But Congress was not so inclined.

The breakthroughs for investors were achieved by a process of whittling rather than from the immediate passage of any legislation. What the big players did throughout the 1990's was to secure exemptions from the CFTC (Commodities Futures Trade Commission). In this way, investment banks and funds found they were able to step over the law until finally unrestricted regulation became an accepted fact of financial life.

GOLDMAN-SACHS WAS the first to get the ball rolling. Goldman realized that it would be much easier to step over the 1936 Commodities Act than to

131   Jerry W. Markham, *Commodity Exchange Act (1936)*, http://www.enotes.com/major-acts-congress/commodity exchange-act

get it revoked, so they bought a small futures trading company by the name of J Aron, and then used their government contacts to win approval from the CFTC to get its new subsidiary exempted from the old trading restrictions. When the exception was granted, Goldman then argued that it should be exempted too since it now owned Aron.[132] The logic seemed clear to the CFTC so they granted Goldman an exemption from the 1936 law as well. As expected, sixteen other large trading firms followed the Goldman route and all received exemptions. Without anyone really noticing or caring to notice, Wall Street had pulled off a complete Coup d'Etat. They had gained the ability to enter into the commodities trade, big time, so big in fact that OPEC's head minister could report that speculators, in the Fall of 2011, had bought oil contracts that were thirty seven times the value of the product they represented. As one would guess, demand like that pushed oil prices up considerably during the months of October and November of that year.

None of this activity has ever received any notoriety. It was all taken care of very quietly. So too was the 1998 rollback of the requirement that if you bought oil, you needed a storage facility to receive delivery. Why was the press so silent on all of this? Matt Taibii of *Rolling Stone*, in recollecting his coverage of the 2008 presidential election provides us with an answer.

---

132   Cho, "A Few Speculators Dominate Vast Market For Oil Trading."

The press, he says, quite simply had no idea of what was going on.[133] Perhaps the same can be said for the entire political establishment.

Covering John McCain in the 2008 presidential election, Taibbi recalls how he and his fellow reporters mocked the Republican candidate for believing that offshore drilling would bring down the high price of oil. After laughing with his fellow reporters at McCain's apparent naiveté, Taibii then recalls asking the question,

> Does anyone here actually know why
> gas prices are going up? I sure
> as hell don't.[134]

Negative chatter followed, indicating to Taibii that none of the reporters covering the 2008 candidates had any idea of what was causing the problem. He observed to a colleague,

> Doesn't that make all of us frauds?
> I mean, if we're covering this stuff
> anyway?[135]

The colleague, seemingly more cynical than Taibii, responded with the surprised question, "You're just finding that out?"

The root of the problem was that the Republican analysis needed to be updated from what had become

---

133   Taibii, *Griftopia, p. 132.*

134   Ibid., p. 127-128.

135   Ibid.

its primordial past. Because of the shortages precipitated by OPEC in the 1970's, the GOP still assumed that rising prices were the result of growing shortages.

The Democrats were no better. They were offering ideas that defied rational analysis. Like the Republicans, they were also tied to old formulations, only in their case, environmental formulations that blamed consumer demand. In the middle of an economic collapse, candidate Obama was assuming the problem grew out of consumer extravagance as he placed the blame on wasteful oil consumption, especially by those who drove SUV's. We needed to mend our ways, he said, presumably by all buying Chevy Volts.[136] For candidate Obama, an environmental position had morphed into an assumption that we were suffering from an excess demand for energy, which we were not. Again, the fact that there was no such supply problem in 2008 hardly altered anyone's thinking. Old formulations, like old habits, die hard.

Apparently neither of the two 2008 candidates realized, nor was honest enough to say, that the real problem came from the speculation that had grown out of government deregulation. Possibly the large campaign donations that each candidate received from Wall Street encouraged them not to look down that alley-way.

THE ENTIRE SUBJECT of government deregulation traces itself back to the Carter administration,

---

136   Ibid.

where the first step in that direction was taken with the airlines. The Reagan administration expanded the trend by beginning the deregulation of oil. The first significant move came when the President began removing price controls at the well head. The oil coming from American wells had been priced according to when the wells were drilled. It was a cumbersome policy that probably needed removing if we ever were going to recover more of our own oil. But unfortunately, it was part of a larger deregulation mentality that led to the removal of the speculative handcuffs that we've mentioned with Goldman and the rest. What started with Reagan as a strategy for solving the supply problem created by OPEC's policy in the 70's ended with the orgy of speculation in 2008 and 2011.

AFTER REAGAN, NOT much happened until Goldman made its move with the CFTC in 1991. Following that, positions established by speculators grew rapidly. Purchases in oil by investment banks and pension funds, both of which often employ hedge funds to make their purchases, jumped, as we've said, from $13 billion in 2003 to the astonishing $260 billion in 2008.[137] A source as unprejudiced as the *Wall Street Journal* noted in 2010, that

> In the market for oil futures and
> options, investors such as hedge funds
> and exchange traded funds have been
> piling into contracts that rise in
> value with prices. As of December 7,

---

137   Ibid.

their bullish bets have exceeded their
bearish bets by about 223 million
barrels, the highest level on record.
<u>In the physical market, oil producers
have ample capacity to keep prices in
check.</u>[underline is mine][138]

Here is a surprisingly upfront statement on the
cause of high oil prices, pointing the finger at speculative demand, not supply. If the quote were from the
NY Times, it would simply elicit a shrug from market
believers along with a clippy "what do you expect from
the *Times*?" But this is from the *Wall Street Journal*,
the major pro-market newspaper in the country.

BESIDES THE ROLLBACK of the 1936 law,
other changes were needed before a trading figure
as extraordinary as the $260 billion number could
be reached. Pension funds, in particular, since they
collectively control more investment money than any
other type of fund, had to be released from the odi-
ous burdens of regulations that specifically forbade
them from investing in commodities. This restriction
was removed in 1994, when the Uniform Prudent
Investors Act was passed. It released pension funds
from the ban on commodities trading. All of the
states followed suit with their own laws, allowing

---

138   Max Whitehouse, "Return of the Rising-Oil –Prices
Peril", Outlook Column, *Wall Street Journal*, December 20,
2010.

their pension funds to begin speculating in commodities.[139] As a result, pension fund money began
to pour into the oil markets after we entered the new
century.

BECAUSE STATE PENSION funds are headed
by people from diverse political backgrounds, these
funds turned to investment banks and hedge funds
to do a large part of their investing. Goldman Sachs,
for instance, created its own index, referred to as the
Goldman Sachs Commodity Index or the S&P/GSCI
to attract pension fund money.[140] Goldman's fund
gives us a good window into the way these institutions
operate. Index speculation allows big banks to invest
funds that go far beyond their own capacity to invest.
In the case of Goldman's fund, pension fund money
deposited in the S&P/GSCI is not invested in oil at
all. What Goldman does is to purchase Treasuries
with the money and invest the interest that's earned
from these Treasuries in oil. This greatly increases
Goldman's ability to place bets in the oil markets.
What they are betting, in essence, is that oil will out-
perform the interest paid by the treasuries. Goldman's
odds are increased along the way because by their
very purchases, they are helping to boost demand,
which in turn drives prices.[141]

---

139   Taibii, *Griftopia*, p. 135.
140   Ibid., pp. 135-136
141   Ibid.

As we've mentioned, the real betting market is in a derivative called a "rate swap." They are not an outright purchase of oil, but rather are side bets placed on oil futures contracts in such huge amounts that contract prices follow the rise of rate swaps prices. Rate Swaps are the concoctions of a rarefied few who trace their lineage back to the 1970's, with the Black-Sholes Model, a model that gave the big banks a new way to calculate the value of complicated derivatives.[142] Complex and esoteric as "rate swaps" may be, their impact on commodities trading is very easy to understand. David Cho describes their significance this way.

> The biggest players on the commodity exchanges often operate as "swap dealers" who primarily invest on behalf of hedge funds, wealthy individuals and pension funds, allowing these investors to enjoy returns without having to buy an actual contract for oil or other goods. Some dealers also manage commodity trading for commercial firms. To build up the vast holdings this practice entails, some swap dealers have maneuvered behind the scenes, exploiting their political influence and gaps in oversight to gain exemptions from regulatory limits and permission to set up new, unregulated markets. Many big traders are active not only on NYMEX but also on private

142   Johnson and Kwak, *13 Bankers,* p. 79.

and overseas markets beyond the CFTC's purview. These openings have given the firms nearly unfettered access to the trading of vital goods, including oil, cotton and corn.[143]

What Cho is alluding to when he speaks of unregulated markets is the creation of new commodities markets for trading that allows speculators to evade what's left of US commodity regulations by trading outside of the NYMEX. In the year 2000, legislation was passed that made it possible to trade oil beyond the NYMEX. The Commodities Futures Modernization Act, otherwise known as the "Enron Loophole," was passed to allow traders to conduct business on private electronic platforms outside the purview of US regulators. The most important of these new centers is in London. Called the ICE or Inter-Continental Exchange, ICE was created by Goldman-Sachs and Morgan Stanley, along with a few other big brokerage firms because the level of frustration among big players over their inability to seize complete control of the NYMEX finally boiled over.[144] These new exchanges gave them the complete control they had been seeking. They would no longer be accountable to even half hearted scrutiny by federal and state regulators. Recall the picture of arrogance presented by the CEO's of the major banks as they testified before the Senate Finance Committee in 2008 after pulling down the entire global economy

---

143   Cho, "A Few Speculators Dominate Vast Market,"
144   Ibid.

with their CDO's (Collateralized Debt Obligations) and you can understand the arrogance that comes with power. These are men now powerful enough to flip off US government regulators should these regulators try to intervene with controls on commodity speculation.

Momentum- The Case of Oil's Rise In 2011

If the argument that prices were driven in 2008 by Wall Street speculators is justified, so too then is it for the spike that began in 2011, a spike that continues right up to this day.

Recall the opening quote in this chapter where hedge fund manager Barton Biggs valued oil at $34/barrel in 2004. Have the fundamentals of the global oil market changed so dramatically since 2004, when prosperity was circling the globe? In 2011 oil was selling at $112/barrel. Has anything happened with the fundamentals to justify this rise? Was there a supply threat from a key supplier like Saudi Arabia or were there threats from OPEC? The answer is no. Just as in 2008, world oil supplies in 2011 were at an all time high, and were guaranteed to be kept that way by the Saudis, who announced just such a policy when the Arab "Spring" uprisings began.

The most that can be said about the political upheavals of 2011 that struck Egypt, Libya, Syria and Bahrain is they were important to the oil markets because trouble in the Middle East always has the potential to make the markets jittery. But there really was no looming supply danger except that the situation provided speculators with an opportunity to establish the momentum they needed to kick off another speculative frenzy. The bad news coming from the streets of the Middle East gave traders the chance to generate a very rapid buildup of oil bets in the rate swaps market. There was little danger in the strategy because political troubles preyed on the long standing belief that high prices are always related to Mid-East shortages. It allowed speculators to establish the momentum in demand that was needed to drive the oil market in the direction they wanted it to go.

Recall the statements made during this period on the radio show, "The Hayes Advantage" where one commentator, a hedge fund manager, said it was the NY Stock Exchange, not consumer demand that determined oil prices. On this same program, another commentator, Steven Short, said the only thing that stopped oil's rise was the hit that investors would take in their other investments when high oil prices began to hurt the other sectors that they were invested in. This led Short to predict that oil wouldn't go beyond $115/barrel. He was right on the mark. Oil went on to reach $113/barrel, and then retreated. As of this writing, Brent Crude, an electronic platform price that most heavily influences our prices, is selling at $109/barrel. Meanwhile the Senate Finance Committee continues to run an occasional dog and pony show for the public, pointing fingers at the oil companies who do not establish the commodity price, while they ignore the findings of their own investigation into oil speculation in 2008.

Even some of the pros have found it difficult to break themselves of the habit of believing in supply/demand fundamentals. Take, for example, the case of Barton Biggs, who heads the successful hedge fund, Traxis.

Biggs recalls an interesting story about value investing (investing by the fundamentals) when his firm shorted oil in 2004. As Biggs describes it,

> our model continued to say that the equilibrium price of oil was somewhere between 28 and 32 a barrel. Inventories were building, OPEC was pumping, and the world economy was slowing . . . .[145]

Warren Buffett himself would have been proud of Biggs short selling oil. He's always argued that investments should be based on fundamentals, and he still does, a fact that makes it unlikely that we'll see him in oil anytime soon.

According to Buffett, people who invest on momentum instead of on fundamentals are prone to hysteria, sometimes seeing ghosts, while at other times seeing the good fairy.[146] We could only wish that investors in oil futures shared Buffet's approach.

To me, said Barton Biggs, Buffet's advice seemed completely sensible, until the price of oil began to take off into the wild blue yonder, losing Traxis a good deal of money. "We were just plain wrong to short", he

---

145   Barton Biggs, *Hedge Hogging*, John Wiley and Sons, Hoboken, NJ, 2006, pp.25-26.

146   Ibid., pp. 26-27.

laments, expecting prices to fall the way the fundamentals dictated that they would.[147]

While Biggs was losing money in 2004 by betting on oil prices falling, a financial piece appeared in the NY Times, criticizing Traxis for putting value over momentum. As Biggs recalls the story,

> A market letter writer who had obviously seen our July letter about Buffet wrote a snide, mocking piece about the folly of being a value investor and how I should have learned by now to buy strength and sell weakness. <u>The disconcerting thing was for that time and that commodity, he was right</u>. [italics mine].[148]

This episode is indeed, as Biggs suggests, disconcerting. Buffett, one of the most successful investors in history, was called archaic by a financial reporter on the staff of the nation's paper of record because he advocated using supply and demand as a guide for investing rather than using market momentum. If the supply of oil and the demand for oil dictated that it should sell for $32/barrel, that information, according to the Times writer was irrelevant. What mattered was that current news events were creating a momentum that would overwhelm the value established by oil's fundamentals, forcing it, in 2008, to $147 and in 2011 to $113. It's not

147   Ibid
148   Ibid., p. 28.

that supply and demand don't count, it's that momentum can and does overwhelm their legitimate market expression if the bets being placed are big enough.[149]

The mere possibility that turmoil in the Middle East could threaten supply is enough to establish an upward momentum because speculators now have the ability to jump on the news.

If we use the image of sharks engaged in a feeding frenzy, it's useful for understanding the oil markets once momentum has been established. Here's how Mallaby describes fund manager Paul Tudor Jones' behavior;

> If Jones' method was to look for
> the trigger that might set off a
> sudden market move, he was also
> willing on occasion to become that
> trigger himself- to jump start a
> reversal in the market trade, so
> initiating a stampede that would
> make his script become reality.[150]

Why are the banks and hedge funds willing to push the momentum envelope? Why are they willing

---

149   One of the most curious discussions to emerge over oil prices in 2008 originated in Paul Krugman's *N Y Times* column. Krugman proposed that the only way prices could have risen from speculation was if speculators had succeeded in hiding vast supplies. Only in this way, he said, could scarcity push prices up. Why he would dismiss the rate swaps market, which releases speculators from having to take possession of oil.is hard to understand.

150   Mallaby, More Money Than God, p. 142

to press consumers with high prices? Consider for a moment the personalities of some of the men who are setting these prices and we get some insight into what the possible answer is.

One of Mallaby's more interesting observations in *More Money Than God* is that many managers are not really grown men yet, at least not in their emotional development. Think about, for example, Ken Griffen, the founder of Citadel Investment Group. Griffen bought himself a $50 million private jet which he had fitted with a crib for his two year old. Or Chris Asness, an irreverent, impatient young man who left Goldman to establish his own fund. He collects and displays plastic super heroes, presumably because like him, they represent the "masters of the universe." Or consider Michael Stienhardt, a hard nosed young man who manages a large, successful firm. After reducing one of his underlings to sobbing, the man blurted out, "all I want to do is kill myself," to which Stienhardt responded, "Can I watch?"[151]

These are not the sort of men that form a sympathetic image of granny sitting in front of her open oven as she tries to keep warm in the winter, or of the average Joe who makes $50,000/year and is spending $75.00/week on gasoline, but they are the men who are setting our oil prices.

THE FORMER CEO of Goldman Sachs and Secretary of the Treasury under President G.W.

151   Ibid., p.4

Bush, Henry Paulson, clearly recognized the danger of these personalities when he recommended that hedge funds be forbidden to short-sell bank stocks in the crises that hung over the nation after Lehman was brought down in the winter of 2008. Like Ben Bernanke, Chairman of the Federal Reserve, and SEC chairman Chris Cox, Paulson feared that hedge funds would bring on a 1930's style depression in 2008 if allowed to.[152] It was a fear not unfounded, for these men had just witnessed the short-selling of Lehman's stock, which caused it to plunge from $16.20/share to $3.65/share, a value so low that it made it impossible for the government to find a buyer for the firm.[153]

What the President and Treasury Secretary feared was that just as the hedge funds took down Lehman, they would take down all the others. This is why, the President reports in his memoirs, they decided to forbid all short selling of bank stocks by hedge funds temporarily, and to go with the Troubled Asset Relief Program (TARP).

IT'S HARD FOR people with average motivations to adjust their thinking to the cold fact that institutions can be so maniacally focused on making money. The fact that high oil prices would wreak havoc with people's personal lives is not a part of the calculation that these firms make when they buy and sell oil on

---

152   George W. Bush, *Decision Points,* New York, Crown Publishers, 2010, p. 456.

153   Ibid.

the NYMEX, or on any of the other newly created electronic platforms that crisscross the globe.

It Can Work Both Ways

We have become so attuned to the possibility of supply problems with oil that we forget that supply is a two way street.

Yes, we've been stung by OPEC, and by the possibility that the Mid-East spigot could be slowed again. These are always possibilities. But the current reality is future oil supplies look brighter, not dimmer than ever. Iraq, for example, is making a big push to go well beyond its past production levels. Today, Iraq's production capacity is at 2.5 million barrels/day (mbd). By 2017, it is expected to be five times that, standing at 12 mbd.[154] And in the US, the breakthroughs in what's called tight oil, oil locked in our vast shale beds, keep coming.

We have already undergone a revolution in natural gas production[155] because of the application of new technologies to shale beds, and now the same applications are being used in the oil industry. In Ohio, for example, an oil rich layer of shale rock called the Utica Shale reserve, "has sparked a leasing frenzy."[156] And, like shale gas, which "has had such a large and sudden impact on

154   "The Great Iraqi Oil rush", *The Wall Street Journal*, March 8, 2011, p. A12.

155   "America's Natural Gas Revolution", *The Wall Street Journal*, November 3, 2009, pp. A20-A21.

156   "Shale Lifts Prospects in Ohio", *The Wall Street Journal*, March 7, 2011, p. A3.

the North American energy scene," tight oil will also probably prove to be revolutionary. And the shale beds extend far beyond the excitement in Ohio. There are shale reserves in North Dakota and Montana, referred to as the Bakken reserves that some have estimated have more oil than the entire Middle East put together.[157] It's hard to say what the actual reserves are, but we do know that since 2003, oil production has been rising rapidly, with the Bakken now producing close to 400,000 barrels/day.[158] There are twenty or so other fields in play.

We are awash in natural gas as well, and for now, at least, it looks like the success we've had with natural gas may also be happening with oil. Shouldn't the Mid-East threat that has haunted us since the 70's be somewhat offset by the optimistic reports on our own reserves? If current prices reflect future pessimism on supply, shouldn't they also reflect future optimism? Why does only bad news seem to influence price? The answer is obvious. For Wall Street, success stories do not allow for the creation of momentum because they rarely come with a sudden news flash. They come with the evolution of new technologies and new techniques. What investors need is the sudden emotional rush created by riots or war. That's what allows for momentum and the making of real money.

There's another reason why good news doesn't trigger a rush of short selling, which would bring

---

157   "Oil- You Better Sit Down", http://bakk

158   "Tight Oil: The Next Energy Gale?" *The Wall Street Journal, March 8, 2011, p.A13.*

down the price. As Barton Biggs describes it in one of his chapter titles, "Short Selling Is Not For Sissies."

One of the problems in selling short is smaller funds don't have the power to move markets. They lack the fire power. So they follow the momentum established by rising prices instead.

> They might know that Japan's equity
> bubble or the mortgage bubble makes
> no sense, but they cannot borrow enough
> to bet against it with the force that
> deflate it.[159] [It's] why finance is
> prone to bubbles.[160] [Why] a trend can
> keep going far beyond the point at
> which it ceases to be rational.[161]

The message is short selling is risky, riskier than buying long. There are, however, a dozen or so hedge funds who have this power;

> If you are a trader with more
> ammunition and courage than the
> rest you can ambush the market
> and jolt it out of its sleepwalk.[162]

Paul Jones, of Tudor Investment Corporation, whom we've already mentioned, made jolting the market by short selling a specialty. In the oil markets

---

159   Mallaby, *More Money Than God,* pp.142-143.

160   Ibid., p. 143.

161   Ibid.

162   Ibid.

in 2008, he proceeded with stealth, placing multiple sell orders once oil had reached stratospheric levels, trying his best not to disturb the upward trend while building his short position. Suddenly Jones switched to his "wild cowboy style", wanting "the market to know that some big swinger is selling."[163]

> 'Offer a thousand!' he yells at his broker. 'No, offer fifteen hundred! Show 'em size! Tell 'em that there's more behind it! Do it! Do it! There's more behind it!'[164]

Jones did drive the price of oil down. His performance produced the stampede out of oil in 2008 just as it was intended to. It quickly settled back to $34/barrel, the price from which it had all started. When it was over, a video caught him pointing to his chest in triumph, signaling it was him that caused the move. Even his own people were blaming the Arabs.[165] This is how oil spirals are really made and then broken.

---

163   Ibid.

164   Ibid.

165   Ibid., p.144.

Chapter 6.
Regulations- We Don't Need Two Thousand Pages

If you want to reform a system
you must do it all at once- like
cutting the tail on a dog. Otherwise
the patient will die.
Gonzalo Sanchez de Lozada- The Bolivian
Finance Minister who broke Bolivia's
hyper-inflation in 1985.

IN THE FIRST five chapters of this book, we argued the case that over the last thirty years the financial sector has dramatically changed the nature of American capitalism, pushing it from a system that could be described as "big firm capitalism" to one that can now best be described as "finance capitalism." We've replaced a system where corporate decision making was based on long term development considerations to one where decisions are made on the basis of immediate profit considerations.

The winners that emerged from this new economic arrangement have obviously been the lords of finance. The losers? Clearly the vast majority of America's middle-class. The question now to be asked is can we reverse this trend, or has the Genie, once let out of the bottle, escaped for all time?

IN OUR OPINION, the trend certainly can be reversed, but it will require political will. First and foremost, it will require the avoidance of complex legislation such as the Dodd-Frank bill because the complexity of legislation like this makes it unenforceable. For example, one part of this two thousand-odd page bill picked up on former Fed chairman Paul Volker's idea that commercial banks be banned from entering into risky trading. To incorporate Volker's ideas into the Dodd-Frank bill, a 298 page proposal was released in October of 2011.[166] Its very length made Volker's proposal obscure, making it an invitation to confusion. Even if commercial banks were of a mind to conform to it, which of course they are not, the question is

> How can banks comply with a rule
> that complicated, and how can
> regulators effectively administrate
> it?[167]

IF REGULATIONS ARE to work, they can neither be too broad nor too vague. What's needed are small, separate bills that target special problems with brevity. All regulations must be clear and to the point.

---

166   "Putting the Clamps on Banks", *Wall Street Journal,* Money and Investing front page, October 12, 2011.
167   Ibid.

Recall that we divided the financial problem into three distinct areas. First, we considered the mergers and acquisition problem, then we discussed the instability caused by opaque asset backed securities. We ended with a discussion of the numerous steps that led to New York's control of the oil markets. Each of these problems must be addressed on their own, with, as we've said, laws that are concise.

Restoring Sanity To the Price of Oil

Let's begin where we ended, with the manipulation of the commodities markets. In the previous chapter we discussed how speculators gained control of oil prices, manipulating demand by executing huge trades in "rate swaps" derivatives in order to drive up the price of legitimate commodities contracts. We found that hedge funds can establish a demand momentum in these markets by purchasing huge amounts of derivatives, often through leveraging. Until the early 1990's this wasn't possible because the Commodities Exchange Act of 1936 deprived speculators of the ability to manipulate price by limiting speculation to approximately 20% of all commodity purchases. This prevented price manipulation while still allowing speculators to eliminate the bottlenecks that could otherwise develop between producers of raw materials and those who process them. This changed in the early 1990's, when the Commodities Futures Trading Commission or CFTC granted wholesale exemptions from the 1936 law, first to Goldman and then to all the other major banks. Nor did the exemptions stop there. In the year 2000, just before he left office, President Clinton made the sixty-four year old commodities act completely obsolete with the passage of The Commodities Futures Modernization Act of 2000, or the CFMA. This new legislation granted Wall Street all the power it needed by permanently deregulating the commodities markets, including commodity derivatives. There had been a struggle over these points within the administration in 1996, after Brooksly Bourne was named the head of the CFTC.[168] This agency, whose prime responsibility is in overseeing commodities trades and derivatives began to warn that the derivatives market was out of control and needed to be reigned in through regulation. Bourne's efforts brought her into direct conflict with Alan Greenspan, Robert Rubin, and Larry Summers. It was a struggle where Bourne was pitted against the administration's chief three heavyweights. Coming from a back-water agency, she never had a chance. The big three fought off any attempt to control the derivatives trade, thereby effectively ending any attempt by government to regulate commodities.[169] The failure also meant that financial contracts written for food and fuel were officially, by the passage of the 2000 act, no longer subject to the 20% rule. It handed over the entire spectrum of commodities and

168   The story is told in detail in *"The Warning"*, a program which appeared on Frontline on Oct 20, 2009.
169   Ibid.

derivatives to speculators, including the hedge funds whose use of leveraging in the buying and selling of commodities could now be used to dramatically influence market demand. Consequently, both food and fuel, the two commodities that make up so much of the middle classes budget, and which play such a large role in insuring the general prosperity of the economy, were placed completely in the hands of speculators. Ominously, it allowed for the wholesale purchases of financial contracts referred to as commodities derivatives. It meant that speculators could sell insurance derivatives (rate swaps) on the original commodities futures contracts that were themselves insurance policies. In other words, a game can now be played that allows hedge funds and big banks to place bets on commodities without limit because this is what these secondary and tertiary derivatives are, betting slips, supposedly providing insurance on insurance contracts. It's a game where the sky is the limit since the common sense notion that insurance policies should actually insure hard assets does not apply. What needs to be done is to put an asset requirement in place in order to limit the number of derivatives that can be written.

How difficult would it be to put such restrictions in place? Very. It would require more than simply reinstating the Commodity Exchange Act of 1936 because with the global expansion of the derivatives markets, we are now dealing with something that extends beyond US borders. For example, under the leadership of Goldman-Sachs, oil is now sold in London on the Intercontinental Exchange (ICE), under the name of Brent crude. Over the past year, Brent's price has frequently risen considerably higher than the price established by NYMEX. This has made Brent the pace setter for oil prices. Consequently, restoring the 20% rule and restricting derivative sales to hard assets would have to be done through international law, which is a daunting prospect. So what's the answer?

The US can go a long way in containing this activity if it treats this kind of electronic speculation the way it treats internet gambling, because in effect, this is what it is. Tax all derivatives not written directly on hard assets heavily. This would prohibit much or all of this activity by banks and hedge funds. The problem is such an action would take an enormous amount of political will, one that could only be generated if there were a genuine public outrage over what's going on. On the part of many, the anger is there. Witness the "Occupy Wall Street" movement. True, it was, in its protest days, a motely group which drew a lot of well-deserved bad publicity. But much of the problem would have disappeared had the group been able to articulate specifically why Wall Street is dangerous and specifically how it can be controlled. The problem with Occupy Wall Street was, and remains, its lack of focus and more specifically, it lack of specific proposals. This is something that can be remedied, a fact that makes a political solution possible..

Besides forcing a political solution, there is always the possibility that oil supplies may eventually overwhelm the ability of traders to control them. It won't be as easy to do as it was with natural gas, because natural gas cannot be shipped on international markets the way oil is. This fact makes it essentially a domestic product. Nevertheless, the current breakthroughs that are being made in bringing tight oil up to the surface does offer the prospect of a long term solution to the high price of oil.

Controlling Mergers and Acquisitions

In Chapter 2, we discussed the problem of the mergers and acquisitions movement that emerged full blown under Michael Milken, and which then became institutionalized with private equity firms. It was noted that this movement has harmed the economy by imposing on corporations a spiraling debt load which has produced diminishing quality in products and services, pressured worker salaries, and now threatens us with corporate bankruptcies. Obviously, this second problem must be dealt with.

CONTROLLING PRIVATE EQUITY firms has to be done with some care because some firms do a lot of their work as venture capitalists, supplying needed funds to young entrepreneurs. Venture capitalist activity should never be interfered with. Unfortunately, however, the other side of venture capitalist firms is the Darth Vader side, where private equity firms execute the leveraged buyouts that wreak such havoc with middle class lives.[170] Presidential candidate, Mitt Romney's equity firm, Bain Capital, is an example of this two-headed hydra problem.[171]

Despite the complexities of private equity firms, it is possible to avoid throwing out the baby with the bath water by imitating what the Europeans and Japanese do.[172] They have been able to control leveraged buyouts very successfully.

The Germans, for example, who refused to become "Americanized", as then Chancellor Gerhard Schroeder put it, passed a number of laws called "poison pills" in order to prevent hostile takeovers. Though American and British investors complained, legislation was passed that has been very effective in preventing leveraged buyouts of German firms by British and American companies.

Poison pill legislation is designed to automatically activate if corporations are faced with a hostile takeover.[173] Such laws, for example, forbid the use of debt acquisition in any attempted buyout. This, of course, is

170   One of the best books available on the operations of venture capitalist firms is Paul Gompers and Josh Lerner, *The Venture Capital Cycle*, Cambridge, MA, The MIT Press, 2002.

171   *The Bain Capital Bonfire*, "Wall Street Journal" Editorial Page, Wednesday, January 11, 2012.

172   Although in the case of the Japanese, their control over leveraged buyouts is automatically achieved by a culture which views this activity as abhorrent.

173   Smith, *The Equity Culture*, p. 293.

a deal killer because takeovers are financed by selling bonds. Also, poison pills can prevent the sale of key assets in a merger deal, preventing the selling off of parts of companies for an immediate profit. There are also poison pills that put restrictions on any layoffs following a possible takeover.[174] Restrictions, such as these, remove most of the incentive for conducting takeovers.

In considering such legislation, we should remember that German leadership is not anti-free market. Under the present Chancellor, Angela Merkel, Germany has moved to adopt a number of market reforms, including tough bargaining with unions and the enactment of flexible labor laws, actions that have helped to make the nation a major force in industrial exports. This illustrates the point that poison pills do not reflect an anti-market mind set. Rather they indicate a common sense approach for controlling a damaging activity.

Regaining Control of the Asset Backed Securities Market.

Recently, an article by Holman Jenkins, one of the editors of the Wall Street Journal, recently criticized the relentless chorus of voices that blame Fannie May and Freddie Mac for the financial meltdown of 2008.[175] In the article, Jenkins points out that the banks could have handled the Fannie/Freddie

---

174   Ibid.

175   Holman Jenkins, *"The Fannie and Freddie Hate Storm: A Dubious Prosecution But It Helps Set the Record Straight,"* Wall Street Journal, December 28, 2011

problem had not major financial institutions lever-aged up in order to buy complex housing derivatives and opaque CDO's. It was the loss of faith in these instruments that clogged the system with unwanted securities and produced a global meltdown.

When even the editorial board of The Wall Street Journal blames asset backed securities for the 2008 collapse, it becomes legitimate to ask why the political right is so obsessed with attacking Fannie Mae and Freddie Mac, and distracting attention from the root cause of the problem. Why do free-market enthusi-asts refuse to discuss the abusive actions that banks are clearly guilty of? Ideology and self interest is the answer. This is why the right turns away and makes it doubly difficult to get reform accomplished. It will be difficult addressing the asset-backed securities prob-lem without the vital support of both political parties and that remains difficult to get. The right needs to recall that all power tends to be abusive, not just gov-ernment power.

LET'S SUGGEST THAT in this area the first thing that needs to be done is to restore stability in our banking system. First and foremost, we need to once again separate commercial banking from investment banking. Commercial banks, which write mortgages, school loans, car loans and the like must be prevented from selling these loans to investment banks, just as they were prior to the 1990's. Denying investment banks these loans would take from them the raw materials they use to manufacture their CDO's. It would also remove from the equation the very thing that encourages commercial banks from loaning to unqualified borrowers.

If we succeed in restoring the historic separation of investment banks and commercial banks, we can immediately remove, with the stroke of a pen, all of the problems that have arisen from the creation of Renieri's Residential Mortgage Backed Securities, the very vehicles that were foremost in bringing down the global house of cards.

We need to gain control of the entire derivatives market as well. We have mentioned this problem with respect to commodities and their association with rising oil prices in particular. But if we are to remove the instability that constantly threatens global markets we need to reign in all derivative sales. Currently they are being written in the hundreds of trillions of dollars because most are written to insure derivatives that already insure against the calamitous effects that currency swings, and interest rate fluctuations can cause.

The sale of financial contracts obviously needs to be limited to the immediate parties that are being protected. Given the unsympathetic nature of governmental advisers on these matters- because most of them are Wall Street people- passing regulations is hard to do. In addition, as we've seen in the case of commodities derivatives, the problem is now global, which means the political likelihood of stiff regulations becomes even more doubtful. This brings us to the obvious conclusion we reached with commodities. We need to tax all derivatives that do not insure hard assets. Either that or get the G-20 to put a ban on them altogether so they can no longer escape the arm of the law.

Summing Up

In a nutshell, taxes need to be imposed on commodities derivatives, poison pills need to be passed to control mergers and acquisitions, and the banking system needs to be separated as it was into a commercial sector and investment sector. In addition, the entire secondary derivatives market needs to be taxed. We need to make speculative gambles on derivatives that are not written on hard assets too risky to take a gamble on.

Throughout this book, we've stressed the belief that the shift in wealth is diminishing the middle class' input into their government. The connection that exists between Washington and Wall Street is now so mutually beneficial that it is breeding a degree of corruption and contempt that governments have for their people in many developing nations.[176]

---

176   The recent revelation that Congress has exempted itself from rules governing insider trader shows just how contemptuous our political leaders have become. For a detailed description of this new form of corruption, see Peter Schweizer, *Throw Them All Out: How Politicians and Their Friends Get Rich off Insider Stock Tips, Land Deals, and Cronyism That would Send the Rest of Us To Prison. Boston: Houghton Mifflin Harcourt, 2011*

The electorate needs to be informed if these problems are to be grappled with. Understanding the situation is a vital first step in building the pressure that is needed to reform the system. It is very distressing to see those people who were serious about reform in the "Occupy Wall Street movement" flailing away without any knowledge of how to address a problem they only vaguely understand. They were pointing their finger in the right direction, but quickly found that impressions are very different from concrete suggestions. We need to change this if we are ever going to get something done.

Bibliography Of Books and Articles Cited

Books

Auerbach, Alan J., ed. *Causes and Consequences.* Chicago: Univ. of Chicago Press, 1988.

Baumol, William, Robert Litan and Carl Schramm. *Good Capitalism/Bad Capitalism: And The Economics of Growth With Prosperity.* New Haven: Yale University Press, 2005.

Biggs, Barton. *Hedge Hogging.* John Wiley and Sons, Hoboken, NJ, 2006.

Bruck, Connie. *The Predator's Ball: The Inside Story of Drexel Burnham and The Rise Of The Junk Bond Raiders.* Penguin Books. New York, 1989.

Bush, George W. *Decision Points.* New York, Crown Publishers. 2010

Drobny, Steven. *Inside The House of Money.* Hoboken, New Jersey: John Wiley and Sons, 2009.

Ehrman, John. *The Eighties: America in the Age of Reagan,* New Haven. Yale University Press, 2005.

Fintan O'Toole, *Ship of Fools: How Stupidity and Corruption Sank the Celtic Tiger,* Public Affairs, Perseus Book Group, 2010.

Fox, Justin. *The Myth of the Rational Market.* Harper Collins Publishers, 2009

Galbraith, John Kenneth. *The New Industrial State.* Boston, Houghton-Mifflin, 3rd. ed. 1967

Gasparino, Charles. *The Sellout: How Three Decades of Wall Street Greed and Government Mismanagement Destroyed the Global financial System.* New York, Harper Collins, 2009.

Gompers, Paul and Josh Lerner. *The Venture Capital Cycle.* Cambridge, MA, The MIT Press, 2002.

Johnson, Simon and James Kwak, *13 Bankers: The Wall Street Takeover and the Next Financial Meltdown.* New York, Pantheon Books, 2010,

Kerouac, Jack. *On the Road. New York: The Viking Press,* 1957.

Kleinknecht, William. *The Man Who Sold The World: Ronald Reagan and the Betrayal of Main Street America.* Nation Books, 2009.

Kosman, John. *The Buyout of America, How Private Equity Will Cause The Next Great Credit Crash. Penguin Group, 2009. P12.*

Krugman, Paul. *The Great Unraveling.* New York: W.W.Norton, 2005

Lambert, Emily. *The Futures, the Rise of the Speculator and the Origins of the World's Biggest Markets.* New York: Basic Books, The Perseus Books Group, 2011.

Letter To Rose Wilder Lane. *Letters of Ayn Rand,* a Dutton Book, 1995

Lewis, Michael. *Liar's Polka.* New York: Norton Paperback, 1987.

Lewis, Michael. *The Money Culture.* New York: Penguin Books. 2011

Lynch, David L. *When The Luck Of The Irish Ran Out.* Palgrave Macmillan, 2010.

Mallaby, Sebastian. *More Money Than God.* New York, The Penguin Group, 2010

Mandrel, Michael. *Economics, The Basics,* McGraw-Hill Irwin, 2009

Meredith, Robyn. *The Elephant and the Dragon: The Rise of India and China and What It Means For All Of Us.* W.W. Norton, 2007.

Mezrich, Ben. *Rigged,* New York, Harper Collins, 2007

Miller, Matt. *The Tyranny of Dead Ideas: Letting Go of Old Ways of Thinking To Unleash A New Prosperity,* Henry Holt and Co., 2010.

Murray, Charles. *In Our Hands: A Plan to Replace the Welfare State,* AEI Press, 2006.

O'Toole, Fintin. *Ship of Fools: How Stupidity and Corruption Sank the Celtic Tiger, Faber and Faber, Ltd., 2009. See especially pp. 127-135.*

Phillips, Kevin. *Bad Money: Reckless finance, Failed Politics, and the Global Crises of American Capitalism,* Viking, The Penguin Group, 2008.

Pickett and Saez, *Income Inequality and US Tax Policy,* Berkley.edu.

Portnoy, Frank. *Fiasco, New York: W.W. Norton,* 2009.

Puzzo, Mario. *The Godfather.* G.P. Putnam's Sons, 1968.
Rand Ayn. *Atlas Shrugged.* New York: Penguin Putnam, 1957.

Rand, Ayn. The Fountainhead, The Bobbs-Merrill Co., 1943.

Rand, Ayn. The Virtue of Selfishness, Signet Printing, 1948.

Reich, Robert. *Supercapitalism,* New York, Vintage Books, 2007

Ricks, Christopher and Willian Vance, eds. *The Faber Book of America,* Faber & Faber, p.362.Smith, B. Mark.

Schumpeter, Joseph. *Capitalism, Socialism and Democracy,* Harper Perennial, 1962.

Schweizer, Peter. *Throw Them All Out: How Politicians and TheirFriends Get Rich off Insider Stock Tips, Land Deals, and Cronyism That would Send the Rest of Us To Prison. Boston: Houghton Mifflin Harcourt. 2011*

Smick, David. *The World Is Curve: Hidden Dangers To the Global Economy, New York: Penguin Group, 2009,* Preface.

Smith, B. Mark. *The Equity Culture, The Story of the Global Stock Marke.,* New York, Farrar, Straus and Giroux, 2003.

Stiglitz, Joseph. *The Roaring Nineties,* New York, W. W. Norton, 2003.

Taibbi, Matt. *Griftopia, Bubble Machines, Vampire Squids, And The Long Con That Is Breaking America.* Spiegel& Grow, New York, 2010. .

Articles

"America's Natural Gas Revolution", *The Wall Street Journal,* November 3, 2009

Cho, David. "A Few Speculators Dominate Vast Market For Oil Trading". *Washington Post,* August 21, 2008.

Commanding Heights. DVD based on a book of the same title "*Corporate Raiders.*" *Business Week,* March 4, 1985.

"Divided We Stand: Why Income Inequality Keeps Rising," OECD, , 2008.

Gini Index in U.S. 1947-2009," Census Bureau, http:// www.census.gov/hhes/www/income/data/ historical/ inequality/f04.xls

"*Gini Index- Income Disparity Since World War II.*" http://en.wikipedia.org/wiki/Gini_ coefficient

Henninger, Daniel. "The Obama Rosetta Stone", *Wall Street Journal,* March 12, 2009.

"*Income Ladder's Sticky Steps*", *The Wall Street Journal,* Saturday/Sunday, November 12-13, 2011

"*Income Levels At The Top*," *Providence Journal,* October 29, 2011, p. C4.

"*Income Inequality Gap Widens*", Wall Street Journal.

"*Japan's Companies gird for Attack*", Wall Street Journal, April 30, 2008, p.A4

Jenkins, Holman. "The Fannie and Freddie Hate Storm: A Dubious Prosecution But It Helps Set the Record Straight." *Wall Street Journal.* December 28, 2011

Markham, Jerry W. "*Commodity Exchange Act*", *(1936)*, E- Notes, http://www.enotes.com/ commodity-exchange-act-1936-   eference/ commodity-exchange-act-1936

Murray, Charles. "A Plan To Replace the Welfare State", Wall Street Journal, March 22, 2006.

Noonan, Peggy. "*An Unserious Speech Misses The Mark*", The Wall Street Journal, January 29-30, 2011, p. A17

Noonan, Peggy. "The Tea Party Movement". *Wall Street Journal*, Op. Ed., October 23, 2010

"Oil- You Better Sit Down", http://bakk *Providence Journal,* October 29, 2011, p. C4.

"Putting the Clamps on Banks", *Wall Street Journal,* Money and Investing section, page 1, October 12, 2011.

Scott, Kenneth and John Taylor, *Wall Street Journal,* "Why Toxic Assets Are So Hard to Clean Up", July, 2009.

Shale Lifts Prospects in Ohio", The Wall Street Journal, March 7, 2011

"Steep Drop Tarnishes Big Bets on Silver", Wall Street Journal, May 4, 2011.

"*Tallying The Toll of US-China Trade*", Wall Street Journal, Sept. 27, 2011.

"The Bain Capital Bonfire." Wall Street Journal. Editorial Page, Wednesday, January 11, 2012.

"*The Great Iraqi Oil Rush*", The Wall Street Journal, March 8, 2011.

"*The Great Misallocators*", The Wall Street Journal, January 26, 2011, p. A18

"*The Raiders.*" Business Week, March 4, 1985.

"*The Warning*". Frontline. Oct.20, 2009.

"*Tight Oil: The Next Energy Gale?*" The Wall Street *Journal, March 8, 2011, p.A13.*

Wallison, Peter. "The Price of Fannie and Freddie Keeps Going Up", WSJ, December 30, 2009.

Whitehouse, Max. "Return of the Rising-Oil –Prices Peril", W*all Street Journal,* December 20, 2010.

Yergin, Daniel and Joseph Stanislaw, *Commanding Heights: The Battle For The World Economy,* A DVD adaptation of the book entitled *Commanding Heights.*

Made in the USA
Charleston, SC
18 July 2015